Theories of Emotion

ALSO AVAILABLE FROM BLOOMSBURY

The History of Emotions: A Student Guide to Methods and Sources,
Katie Barclay

Thinking Through Loneliness, Diane Enns

A Cultural History of the Emotions, ed. Susan Broomhall,
Jane W. Davidson and Andrew Lynch

*The Bloomsbury Research Handbook of Emotions in Classical Indian
Philosophy*, ed. Maria Heim, Chakravarthi Ram-Prasad and Roy Tzohar

Theories of Emotion

Expressing, Feeling, Acting

Pia Campeggiani
Translated by Enrico Zoffoli

BLOOMSBURY ACADEMIC
LONDON • NEW YORK • OXFORD • NEW DELHI • SYDNEY

BLOOMSBURY ACADEMIC
Bloomsbury Publishing Plc
50 Bedford Square, London, WC1B 3DP, UK
1385 Broadway, New York, NY 10018, USA
29 Earlsfort Terrace, Dublin 2, Ireland

BLOOMSBURY, BLOOMSBURY ACADEMIC and the Diana logo are trademarks
of Bloomsbury Publishing Plc

First published in 2021 in Italy as Introduzione alla filosofia delle emozioni
by Clueb

First published in Great Britain 2023

Cover design: Jess Stevens
Cover image: *Les 400 coups* (© Cocinor)

A catalogue record for this book is available from the British Library.

A catalog record for this book is available from the Library of Congress.

ISBN: HB: 978-1-3502-9792-0
PB: 978-1-3502-9791-3
ePDF: 978-1-3502-9790-6
eBook: 978-1-3502-9794-4

Typeset by Deanta Global Publishing Services, Chennai, India
Printed and bound in Great Britain

To find out more about our authors and books visit www.bloomsbury.com and
sign up for our newsletters.

For Douglas

Contents

Part III

Figures

About this book

This book provides a philosophical introduction to the most influential theories of emotion of the past sixty years in philosophy, psychology and biology. It features an introductory chapter on definitions of emotion, followed by three main parts on the way emotions are expressed, subjectively experienced and related to action and motivation. Taking a multidisciplinary and empirically informed perspective, the general approach integrates philosophical analysis with the discussion of cutting-edge research in psychology and cognitive science, contextualizing current debates in the history of ideas from Darwin to pragmatism.

The introductory chapter provides an entry point to the varied landscape of contemporary emotion studies. Emotion researchers, some say, face a scandal: there is no agreement on what emotion is. Theories differ wildly in their identification of emotion's defining feature(s). This chapter investigates the nature of definitional disagreements, exploring their theoretical assumptions and offering viable alternatives. Specifically, it considers whether emotions are natural kinds and distinguishes between descriptive and prescriptive approaches to emotion. It reviews the debate between classical and prototype theories of categorization and explores the potential of conceptual metaphor theory to reveal (and jettison) implicit essentialist assumptions. Its main upshot is the rejection of an object-based view of emotions as psychic items that can be broken down into constituent parts in favour of a holistic approach to emotional experiences as at once expressive, phenomenal and pragmatic phenomena.

The philosophical analysis developed in the introductory chapter is complemented by the examination, at the beginning of each part, of the work of one of three of the most important historical figures in the development of emotion theory, namely Charles Darwin, William James and John Dewey. All too often, the contribution of these foundational thinkers has been only partially appreciated and their appeal to a holistic, organic approach to emotion has regularly been overlooked. Building on their groundbreaking intuitions, the three parts illustrate their legacy in contemporary thinking and how a careful and unbiased reading of their work can further enrich it.

Part I, on Expression, is devoted to Darwin and the contemporary reception of his ideas on evolution and the unity of humankind. It surveys the theories of emotion that have been proposed by evolutionary psychologists Leda Cosmides and John Tooby, by psychologists Paul Ekman and Carroll Izard, and by neuroscientist Jaak Panksepp. A presentation of Basic Emotion Theory is followed by a discussion of the so-called unity/disunity debate, that is the debate regarding whether basic emotions are the only 'genuine' ones or serve as building blocks of secondary emotional processes. The idea that basic emotions are innate, biologically inherited and, therefore, relatively immune to linguistic and cultural influences has been strongly attacked by psychological and cultural constructionists. Part I includes a presentation of this criticism, discussing Schachter and Singer's cognition-arousal theory, James Russell's work on core affect and Lisa Barrett's conceptual act theory.

Part II, on Experience, is dedicated to so-called 'feeling theories', starting with that proposed by William James and including Antonio

Damasio's somatic theory. Part II also features a section dedicated
to the cognitivist approach that flourished in the 1960s and 1970s
as a reaction to traditional feeling theories and their neglect of the
world-relating intentional properties of emotions. A discussion of
the intentionality of emotions and the relation between emotions and
values as their formal objects is followed by the presentation of the
appraisal theories advanced by Magda Arnold and Richard Lazarus
and of Klaus Scherer's componential model. Robert Solomon's
evaluative judgement theory is also discussed, as well as perceptual
theories such as those of Jesse Prinz, Peter Goldie and Christine
Tappolet.

Part III, on Action, is dedicated to John Dewey's insights on emotion
and the 'organic circuit' and to those contemporary theories that
emphasize emotion's motivational dimension. Nico Frijda's notion
of 'action tendencies' is presented, together with Andrea Scarantino's
motivational theory and Deonna and Teroni's attitudinal theory.
A final section deals with the new approaches associated with 4E
(embodied, embedded, extended and enacted) cognition, especially
enactivism. Discussion of Jesse Prinz's most recent work on emotion
is followed by a sketch of Daniel Hutto's teleosemiotic account and
an illustration of Giovanna Colombetti's proposals on enactive and
extended affectivity. Paul Griffiths and Andrea Scarantino's work on
emotion and affordances is also considered.

Besides providing a theoretical introduction to different approaches in contemporary emotion theory, the book puts them to the
test, featuring three sections that review current discussions of the
role of emotions in social cognition, decision-making and aesthetic
experience, respectively.

'Debate I: The Emotions of others' poses the following
questions: What is the relation between emotional expressions and
corresponding mental states? Are they just the visible consequences

of inner and invisible processes or are these two dimensions, the inner and the outer, inextricably interconnected, as Darwin believed? Does the meaning of expression and behaviour derive from the mental states by which they are caused or are they endowed with intrinsic psychological meaning? In the theory of mind debate, different approaches provide different answers. Debate I focuses on the main theories that have been proposed in order to explain how we can understand what other people feel. It illustrates theory theories, simulation theories and theories of direct social perception, and discusses the phenomena of facial feedback and emotional contagion.

'Debate II: Sense and sensibility in decision-making' asks whether, when we make a decision, we should keep a cool head or follow our heart. Discussing Damasio's somatic marker hypothesis and Tversky and Kahneman's psychophysics of value, it shows that we do not really have a choice: decision-making processes are always and inevitably underpinned by emotions, for good and for ill.

Finally, 'Debate III: Emotions towards fictional entities' deals with the place of emotions in aesthetic response. In contemporary philosophical theorizing, one issue, in particular, seems to have become a recalcitrant problem: when engaging with works of fiction, we experience emotions about states of affairs that we know do not exist. Is this rational? In fact, is it even possible? Debate III discusses the relation between emotions, real life and imagination, showing how enactivist accounts of emotion are best suited to provide cognitively realistic explanations of emotions towards fictional characters.

Emotion research is a booming field and an introductory book can hardly cover all the relevant topics and issues. Nonetheless, by presenting the main ideas discussed in contemporary debates and by promoting an understanding of their historical origins and development, this book aims to provide students and scholars in different disciplines with what is needed to start learning about emotion.

Acknowledgements

While writing this book, I have received feedback and support from Roberto Brigati, Douglas Cairns, Fausto Caruana, Giovanna Colombetti, Valentina Petrolini, Andrea Scarantino, Fabrice Teroni and Marco Viola. Fabrice and Marco have generously provided me with detailed and insightful comments on the manuscript. Douglas has also helped me check the final draft of the English version.

Many other people have helped me in the research with comments, valuable discussions and reading suggestions. I am particularly grateful to Noga Arikha, Guido Baggio, Marta Caravà, Eric Cullhed, Sara Dellantonio, Vittorio Gallese, David Konstan, Karin Kukkonen, Gloria Origgi, Giuliano Pancaldi, Jean-Alexandre Perras, Matteo Santarelli, Vincenzo Reale and Curie Virag.

My parents, my sister and my brother-in-law deserve special acknowledgement for their encouragement and care.

Finally, I should like to thank the University of Bologna, Italy, for financial support towards the English translation of this volume.

What I know of emotions, and how to study them, I have learnt from Douglas Cairns: this book is for him.

Introduction

Defining emotions

The English word 'emotion' comes from the French *émotion* which, in turn, originates from the verb *émovoir*. Occurrences of this verb (in the form *esmoveir*, from vulgar Latin *exmovere*) are attested in ordinary French from the eleventh century onwards, when it was used in its literal sense of 'moving' or 'initiating movement'. It acquired the transferred meaning of 'stirring passions' more or less a century later. As for the noun *émotion*, it appeared in the fifteenth century and for 100 years its principal meaning was that of 'uprising', 'civil unrest' or 'agitation'. In the seventeenth century it began to be used in connexion with physical disturbance and turmoil (e.g. due to an illness or to love) and it acquired its current meaning of 'subjectively experienced affective state' soon thereafter.[1]

It was right about that time, in the mid-seventeenth century, that the French *émotion* entered other European languages, but it did so carrying its original semantic value. In Castilian, *emoción* had the principal meaning of 'uprising' and 'agitation' until the nineteenth century, when it is first attested in the sense of *animi perturbatio*.[2] In Italian, *emozione* acquired its current meaning only in the second half of the eighteenth century, but it was only after the end of the fascist period that language purists ceased to oppose its use.[3] In German, too, *Emotion* shifted from the meaning of 'civil uprising' in the seventeenth century to that of 'inner turmoil' in the eighteenth century. Still, the term *Gefühl* remained dominant both in ordinary and philosophical language and *Emotion* has gained common currency only in recent decades. As for English, the initial, generic sense of 'agitation' or 'state of excitement' that is attested in the seventeenth century developed into the current, more specialized meaning only 200 years later,[4] when the established vocabulary of psychology also changed and came to subsume the older categories of 'passions' and 'affections' in the new one of 'emotions'.[5]

The language of 'emotion' as such, therefore, is a relatively recent addition to European mindsets and vocabularies. This can appear surprising. After all, emotions are ubiquitous in our daily lives, as prominent in neuroscience laboratories and academic research as in the emoji keyboard of our phones and Pixar animated movies. But what appears even more surprising is that researchers do not share a common definition of 'emotion' because they disagree significantly about what emotions actually are. An examination of the reasons for this disagreement will provide us with a good entry point to contemporary emotion research.

Many theories, many definitions

Odyssey, twentieth book. Disguised as a beggar and covered by a cloak, Odysseus lies in the vestibule of the Royal Palace of Ithaca, where he has returned after twenty years. His home and his wife are besieged by the suitors, who are feasting and celebrating with his disloyal handmaidens, oblivious to the vengeance that is about to come upon them. Odysseus,

> intending evils in his heart for the suitors, / lay awake there, as those women were coming / from their hall, the ones who mixed with the suitors before, / providing merriment and laughter for each other. / His heart stirred in his dear chest, / and he pondered

hard, in his mind and in his heart, / whether to rush after them and make death for each of them / or let them mix with the haughty suitors / a last and final time, and his heart growled inside him. / As a dog stands over her tender puppies / and growls at a man she doesn't recognize, eager to do battle, / so it growled inside him in indignation at their evil actions, / then pounded his chest and scolded his heart: / 'Endure for now, my heart. You once endured another even worse thing, / on that day when the Cyclops, irresistible in fury, / ate my mighty comrades. You endured it, until cunning / led you from the cave, though you thought you'd die'. / So said he, accosting the dear heart in his chest, / and, in strict obedience, his heart remained constantly enduring, / but he himself tossed to and fro. (*Odyssey* XX, 5-24; trans. Huddleston)

In reading these verses, many philosophers of emotions would deconstruct the narrative by identifying some core aspects of Odysseus' emotional experience. The perception of a stimulus, represented here by the laughter of the betraying handmaidens, fuels Odysseus' anger. The thought of insult and injustice, along with the picture of the suitors threatening Penelope and squandering his possessions, is accompanied by powerful physical alterations, which Homer describes with evocative metaphors revolving around Odysseus' feelings – his spirit stirred in his chest, while his heart (i.e. the fury of anger) growled like a dog. Odysseus is about to give in to his lust for revenge, as he feels the urge to pounce on those women and kill them. And yet he knows he must wait. He reminds himself of how he was able to endure even more atrocious ordeals in the past, and thus subdues his anger.

Perceptions, thoughts, physical symptoms and feelings, desires, impulses to action, modulation of memories and expectations – which of these aspects (a philosopher would ask) is the one that truly defines

Odysseus' emotion? Does any of these elements constitute a necessary feature, in the absence of which an episode could not be considered to be an emotional one? Or is it perhaps the case that emotions consist of a combination of all these elements? Different theories propose different definitions, depending on which component they deem essential to the concept of emotion.[6] For example, some tend to regard subjective sensations as the distinguishing element of emotions, while others focus on the relationship that links emotions with values (i.e. on the process of evaluating the circumstances that elicited them); yet others define emotions in terms of a motivational drive to engage in certain courses of action.[7]

We will have the opportunity below to review the different takes on this issue in contemporary debate and to assess their strengths and weaknesses. Before getting started, however, a preliminary clarification is in order, which concerns the question of whether it even makes any sense to embark on a quest for a *definition* of emotion.

Categorization is not a matter to be taken lightly

Traditionally, a category is defined with reference to a set of properties that are shared by each of its members and that each of the members possesses for intrinsic reasons. If this is the case, then we are committed to the view that x is a member of category C if and only if x presents the essential and defining characteristics of C. Whether or not we recognize these characteristics is irrelevant to the existence of the category itself, for this amounts to an objective fact of the world by virtue of the properties inherent in its members. On the face of it, all this seems quite straightforward. Still, as George Lakoff reminds us, 'categorization is not a matter to be taken lightly' (Lakoff 1987: 5).

The major problems lurking beneath the traditional account were first spotted by Ludwig Wittgenstein. In his *Philosophical*

Investigations, published posthumously in 1953, he introduced the notion of 'family resemblances' to show that categories such as GAME, far from being defined by a set of properties shared by each member, include elements that are similar in a wide variety of ways. Consider for instance the games of chess, poker, volleyball and children's role-playing games: not all of them are strategy games, nor do they all fall into the category of team games; poker players compete for victory, whereas in children's role games there are often neither losers nor winners; some people play for fun, others do so as they engage in sporting activities, others play as professionals and so on. Moreover, not only is the category of GAME not defined by the possession, on the part of its members, of a specific collection of characteristics; it is also worth noting that its boundaries are elastic, as they can be stretched to include even further games, as long as these display some adequate similarities with the elements that are already included as members. This is the case, for example, of numbers – as we can see with reference to integers, rational, real or complex numbers.

Categories are not separated from each other by natural boundaries, and in most cases the question cannot even be couched in the terms of an inside–outside divide:[8] it is thanks to the pioneering research of cognitive psychologist Eleanor Rosch that we can now embrace a comprehensive theoretical perspective, backed by substantial experimental evidence, on the problem of categorization. The virtue of Rosch's view is that it helps us identify and illustrate two phenomena that it would be otherwise impossible to explain on the basis of the classical approach to categories: first, if it were true that categories are defined by the set of properties shared by their members, then a category should be exemplified to the exact same degree by each of its members. But this is not the case: with the notion of 'prototypes', Rosch has shown that there are in fact better and worse examples of any category. For example, for most North Americans sparrows and robins are more representative of the category of BIRDS than penguins or emus (Rosch 1975). Some kinds of fruit, such as apples and pears, are prototypical examples of that category. Cherries are a good example, while coconuts are not particularly representative. The category of FRUIT has an internal structure because its inclusion mechanism works by degrees, and not by identifying a stable set of characterizing properties and excluding the elements that lack such properties. In addition, the category of FRUIT is not defined by clear-cut boundaries, and may in fact overlap with neighbouring categories such as VEGETABLES. Thus, while from a botanical point of view a courgette is indeed a kind of fruit, from a practical and contextual point of view (i.e. from the perspective of a person preparing their dinner) it seems to have more in common with lettuce and spinach than with oranges.

Second, as Rosch observed, if the members of a category were intrinsically and objectively fitted with the set of properties that entitle them to belong in that category, regardless of the categorizer, then no physical, psychological, social or cultural characteristics of the latter should interfere with the specification of those properties. Rosch has shown, however, that category formation heavily depends on a number of factors that play a key role from a functional and epistemological perspective, including neurophysiology, sensorimotor capacities and the potential for interaction afforded by the environment, as well as the ease of cognitive processing in terms of mnemonics, learning, recognition and communication (e.g. Rosch 1978). Consequently, though at first sight they seem to be inherent in external reality, the attributes that we perceive as characterizing the basic level of our conceptual categories actually emerge from the way we interact with external reality itself – through our motor programmes, our visual capacities, our cultural priorities and our purposes.[9]

Brent Berlin and Paul Kay have provided a perfect example of how the properties of certain categories are determined by the biological capacities and physical and cultural experience of human beings. In 1969 they published a book entitled *Basic Color Terms* in which they illustrated two surprising discoveries. The first was that although different languages employ significantly different terms to indicate colours, there are ways of subdividing the colour spectrum that are more natural than others. Despite cultural differences and regardless of the available vocabulary, speakers of different languages make similar choices when it comes to choosing the most representative shade within a certain colour area. The so-called focal colours are the shades that best exemplify their category and are associated with what Berlin and Kay called 'basic color terms'. The second discovery concerned the acquisition of these basic colour terms in different languages – which occurs according to a predictable pattern. When a language has only two basic colour terms, these are always black and white: the latter includes white, yellow, orange and red, while the former comprises black, blue, green and grey. The third basic colour term is red, followed by yellow, blue or green. The fifth colour is brown, followed in the sixth position by purple, pink, orange or grey. The set of universal focal colours is determined by human beings' neurophysiological structure, and, more specifically, by the mechanism through which the three different types of retinal cells (i.e. the cones, which have absorption peaks at different wavelengths and absorption spectra that largely overlap with each other) absorb light and thus detect colours. Within the broad constraints imposed by the perception of focal colours, specific cultural orientations also come into play, in the form of heterogeneous interpretations of boundaries between colour shades that lead to the lexicalization of different colour categories depending on the actual communication needs. Research on colour perception clearly shows that categories do not exist independently of us, that is of our biological, social and cultural constitution.

Rosch's theory led to a reformulation of several concepts that are key to cognitive psychology, including that of EMOTION. Beverly Fehr and James Russell (1984) showed that the common-sense category of EMOTION (and the categories related to individual emotions) has an internal structure that lacks clear-cut boundaries and includes elements that can be more or less apt to exemplify it. Fear, anger, love and happiness exemplify the concept of emotion more effectively than – say – admiration, boredom or relief. Then there are ambiguous cases: if the boundaries of the category of EMOTION were precisely defined, then both its central and more peripheral members would unequivocally fall within them, and yet ordinary speakers do not qualify 'respect' and 'modesty' as emotions as often and as immediately as they do with 'joy' or 'sadness'. In other words, the phenomena we commonly refer to as 'emotions' certainly exist, but this does not imply that it is possible to give a correct, unequivocal and inclusive definition of the multiple forms in which they occur. This means that a theory of emotions that aspires to fit as much as possible within the pre-theoretical intuitions of ordinary speakers will have to consider carefully whether or not it is appropriate to define emotions by reference to a set of essential properties and necessary conditions for membership.

Some philosophers and psychologists start from the assumption that the category of EMOTION and its subordinate categories related to specific terms such as FEAR or LOVE are natural kinds, which means that they should be treated as classes of phenomena that can be objectively identified and whose existence does not ultimately depend on the arbitrariness of our linguistic, social and cultural usages, as well as on the grounds that they share some common properties or a common cause.[10] Consider for example Paul Ekman's theory, which identifies a class of basic, universal and innate emotions, namely anger, disgust, fear, happiness, sadness and surprise.[11] Each basic emotion (which does not consist in a single affective state, but rather encompasses a family of similar states) corresponds to an 'affect program', that is to a pattern of coordinated physiological, autonomic, neural, behavioural and expressive reactions. In Ekman's view, Basic Emotion Theory identifies the essence of emotions and makes it possible to draw a clear line between emotions proper and other affective states: 'An emotion is either basic, or it is another affective phenomenon saturated with but different from the emotions, such as a mood, an emotional trait, an emotional disorder, etcetera' (Ekman and Cordaro 2011: 365). Some, however, have pointed out that Ekman's theory does not permit a proper understanding of those emotions that require processing complex information in a sophisticated manner, as may be the case with envy or shame.[12] It has also been observed that there is little empirical evidence in support of Ekman's hypothesis according to which specific emotions (such as 'anger') display some distinctive facial expressions that constitute essential elements of his definition of 'anger' (Barrett 2006; Barrett et al. 2019). Consequently, according to Ekman's essentialist approach, all those instances that an ordinary speaker would define by appealing to the emotion of anger, but which do not occur together with any of the expected facial expressions, are not really instances of anger. Similarly, Ekman is committed to arguing that grief is not an emotion, but rather an 'emotional plot', which lasts longer than sadness and is more specific to the kind of loss that the subject has endured (Ekman 1992).

In short, prescriptive definitions can be conducive to illustrating certain aspects of emotions, in that they can help flesh out possible correlations, draw general conclusions on the results obtained and formulate predictive hypotheses on the basis of major similarities and shared characteristics. However, we must bear in mind that if we rely on a definition based on the identification of essential common properties, that is on a classical approach to categorization, we cannot account for common-sense categories or for the entire spectrum of available empirical data, thus failing to fully appreciate the phenomenological complexity of emotions on the level of experience. According to James Russell, scholars working on emotions are faced with a 'scandal', namely the lack of agreement about what an emotion is.[13] Perhaps, though, instead of persisting in the search for such a convergence point, we should acknowledge that the scandalous lack of any viable definition of emotion is a characteristic feature of the phenomenon we are investigating and not an obstacle in the path towards its understanding.[14]

Abstract concepts are mostly metaphorical

Metaphors are of crucial importance when it comes to the formation of concepts, including that of emotion. In *Metaphors We Live By*, published in 1980, linguist George Lakoff and philosopher Mark Johnson showed that a metaphor is not merely a rhetorical device deployed at the level of language, but a fundamental feature of thought and cognition that informs the ways in which we see and understand the world. Let us consider, for example, the concept of ARGUMENT and the conceptual metaphor ARGUMENT IS WAR, which in ordinary language is articulated in expressions such as 'your claims are indefensible', 'I attacked every weak point in your argument', 'your criticism is right on target', 'I demolished your argument' and so on. Lakoff and Johnson note that this has to do not only with the way we speak, but also with our behaviour and with what we pay attention and attach importance to: we plan our argumentative strategies, we defend our ideas and we are more inclined to consider our interlocutor as an adversary rather than as someone who is spending time to search for some common ground. A similar line of reasoning applies to the conceptual metaphor TIME IS MONEY, which emerges from expressions such as 'don't waste your time', 'my time is valuable', 'it's a good way to spend your time', 'I've invested a lot of time in this project' and so on. We perceive time as a valuable commodity: we are paid by the hour, we buy minutes of phone credit, we pay hotels depending on the duration of our stay and so on. This is a typically Western and relatively recent concept, stemming from the social and economic evolution that has shaped our culture. There are many ways of conceptualizing time and other cultures have developed different metaphors.

The core thesis upon which the conceptual metaphor theory hinges is that metaphors allow us to understand and experience something in terms of something else. In particular, conceptual metaphors establish a relation between two distinct domains, one of which is typically more concrete than the other: it thus becomes possible to 'map' the domain with which we are more familiar onto the more abstract concept. Orientational metaphors, for example, exploit some reference to our bodily experience to give a spatial orientation to abstract concepts: thus, by virtue of our upright posture, which determines a high and a low, we feel down when we are ill or sad and we fall into depression or sleep; on the contrary, we feel up to doing what we have the energy to do, we wake up in the morning and we can be at the peak of physical fitness. Similarly, as a consequence of the bilateral symmetry that separates the ventral side from the dorsal one, thus specifying a front and a back, we think of the future as being ahead of us (and we move towards it) and of the past as being behind us (and we move away from it).[15] Orientational metaphors show that we understand the world based on the way we move our body; generally speaking, a conceptual metaphor makes it possible to understand an abstract concept by virtue of the experiential aspects in which it is rooted.

As documented by Zoltán Kövecses (2000), many of the terms and descriptions that refer to emotions are figurative (i.e. metaphorical and metonymic). A particularly important role is played here by the physiology of emotional experience, such as when we 'shiver with fear', when we are 'fuelled with anger' or when we 'burn with love' for somebody. The link between the physical symptoms, expressions of emotions and figurative language helps us introduce a second preliminary question to our review of contemporary emotion theories – a question that is in some ways related to the difficulties we have addressed in the previous section concerning the plausibility of definitions. We may call this 'the problem of reifying thought'.

As Lakoff and Johnson have noted, a key method that helps us verbalize, categorize, quantify and, in general, reflect on our experience consists in conceiving of it in terms of discrete physical entities, such as objects or substances. With these ontological metaphors of entity and substance, we can fulfil a wide spectrum of needs, as they allow us to refer to ideas, values, thoughts and, of course, emotions (e.g. 'your fear of speaking in public is a major obstacle for your career'), to indicate their intensity or scope (e.g. 'it takes a lot of courage to accomplish this'), to illustrate causal links or motives (e.g. 'he hit him out of anger', 'I turned my life around because I wasn't happy') and so on. A further type of ontological metaphor, called 'container metaphor', emerges from the fact that being embodied leads us to organize our actions and our knowledge in terms of what is inside or outside us. We conceive of ourselves as 'containers' within which our subjective experience unfolds. Emotions are inside us, but, at the same time, they become themselves containers in which we fit, as when we are 'in love' or we live 'in hope'. Either way, whether they are located in our inner selves or whether we are contained in them, emotions are equated with physical objects. Consequently, we tend to attribute to them specific parts, components or aspects that, by metonymy, stand for the emotion as a whole: this is the case when we 'shiver' (with fear) or when 'our blood boils' (due to anger) and, more generally, when we describe our emotional state by referring to the symptoms it causes (e.g. when we are 'drunk with power' or 'madly in love').

Ontological metaphor seems to be the main tool we employ to characterize and conceptualize our subjective experience: when we 'have an idea or a desire', when 'a thought pops up in our mind' or when we are 'struck by a feeling', we conceive of ideas, desires, thoughts and feelings as macrophysical entities located in space and time, which are themselves capable of acting and driving our actions (personification being another kind of ontological metaphor). This tendency is so deep-seated in our cognitive systems that most of the time we are not even aware that we are resorting to metaphorical structures. However, whereas in the realm of common-sense and ordinary communication this lack of awareness is generally harmless, in philosophy and psychology it becomes the main source of what may be called the 'problem of reifying thought', that is, of an approach that considers subjective experiences, including emotions, as psychical 'objects' consisting of several 'parts' and endowed with determinable, locatable and measurable 'properties', and, on some accounts, reducible to underlying physical mechanisms, or to patterns that may be fully explained in sheer physical terms.

Understanding the mechanism of conceptual metaphor helps us resist the reifying temptation to separate external reality from the internal one, in which emotions are supposed to be located. We can thus get rid of the idea that emotions are discrete entities which can be broken down into different parts (some of which are more essential than others) and which are related to other physical 'objects' according to some linear sequence (such as the sequence relied upon in common-sense psychology: stimulus→ interpretation of stimulus → emotion → physiological alteration → bodily feelings). We thus need not relinquish our belief that emotions are real, and at the same time we are not committed to the reductionist thesis that what is real is physical and can be fully explained on the physical level. In short, this approach allows us to fit emotions into the broader picture of our experience as a network of bodily, practical and evaluative interactions – not as things to be identified, located and broken down.

Part I

Expression

Darwin

In addition to other notebooks and manuscripts left by Darwin after his return from the Beagle voyage, the Darwin Archive at the Cambridge University Library hosts the so-called *Notebook M.* Bound in a red leather cover, this manuscript has a cream-coloured label on the front that contains the letter *M* and the word *Expression.* Here, during the summer of 1838 Darwin wrote down his thoughts on the biological origins of behaviour, but also dealt quite extensively with the expression of emotions – a topic to which he later devoted his famous essay *The Expression of the Emotions in Man and Animals* (1872). Many of the lines of research developed in the 1872 text already appeared in draft form in *Notebook M.* These include in particular the interpretation of the expression of emotions in evolutionary terms, that is as the legacy of a response that was originally conducive to the adoption of behavioural patterns geared to cope with certain environmental stimuli. This is important: Darwin never claimed that expressions evolved in order to communicate emotions. Although he acknowledged that expressions play a crucial communicative role, insofar as they are interpreted as 'signs' by the observer, his core claim was that this role emerged only as a secondary effect: 'every true or inherited movement of expression seems to have had some natural and independent origin. But once acquired, such movements may be

voluntarily and consciously employed as a means of communication'
(Darwin [1872]2009: 351).

In the introduction to *The Expression of the Emotions in Man
and Animals*, Darwin reviewed the main findings on gestures and
expressions available at the time and pointed out that no one before him
had undertaken to collect and interpret data in the light of the theory
of evolution. In Darwin's view, the main obstacle to understanding
the cause and origin of expressions in humans and other animals is
the belief that species (including humans) are immune to change,
coupled with the tendency to consider each species in isolation:

> No doubt as long as man and all other animals are viewed as
> independent creations, an effectual stop is put to our natural desire
> to investigate as far as possible the causes of expression. By this
> doctrine, anything and everything can be equally well explained;
> and it has proved as pernicious with respect to expression as
> to every other branch of natural history. With mankind some
> expressions, such as the bristling of the hair under the influence
> of extreme terror, or the uncovering of the teeth under that of
> furious rage, can hardly be understood, except on the belief that
> man once existed in a much lower and animal-like condition.
> The community of certain expressions in distinct though allied
> species, as in the movements of the same facial muscles during
> laughter by man and by various monkeys, is rendered somewhat
> more intelligible, if we believe in their descent from a common
> progenitor. He who admits on general grounds that the structure
> and habits of all animals have been gradually evolved, will look
> at the whole subject of expression in a new and interesting light.
> (Darwin [1872]2009: 19)

In a letter to Alfred Russel Wallace in March 1867, Darwin was
quite explicit about his own intentions: 'I want, anyhow, to upset

Sir C. Bell's view . . . that certain muscles have been given to man solely that he may reveal to other men his feelings' (Marchant 1916: 182).[1] Charles Bell (1774–1842) was a Scottish surgeon, anatomist and neurologist whose lectures at the Medical Faculty of Edinburgh University Darwin had attended. Much of the scientific knowledge of the time in the field of emotions was built around Bell's ideas, until Darwin challenged their assumptions with the publication of *The Expression of the Emotions in Man and Animals*. In 1811 Bell had published a short treatise on neurology entitled *Idea of a New Anatomy of the Brain*, in which he emphasized, among other things, that the anterior root of spinal nerves transmits efferent motor impulses, and thus serves a different function from the posterior one, which transmits afferent sensory impulses. Bell was also the author of the beautiful engravings contained in his *The Anatomy of the Brain, Explained in a Series of Engravings* (1802), as well as of the drawings (also later engraved) collected in *A Series of Engravings, Explaining the Course of the Nerves* (1803). But it was his essays, published in the volume entitled *Essays on the Anatomy of Expression in Painting*,[2] that most influenced Darwin's work on the expression of emotions. Here Bell proposed an anatomical study of expressions, and, from the second edition, an analysis of the role played by the nervous system in their generation. Bell was a creationist and claimed that the great variety of facial expressions of which humans are capable is due to the presence of muscles that are absent in other animals and with which God endowed only humans, so that they could express and communicate their states of mind.[3] Darwin finds this view untenable: 'Actions, which were at first voluntary, soon became habitual, and at last hereditary, and may then be performed even in opposition to the will. Although they often reveal the state of mind, this result was not at first either intended or expected' (Darwin [1872]2009: 352). His determination to challenge the idea that God endowed humans with more complex facial musculature than other animals in order to enable them to communicate their emotions is probably the reason why Darwin paid relatively little attention to the communicative function of expressions.[4]

In *The Expression of the Emotions in Man and Animals*, Darwin aimed primarily to describe those bodily expressions and movements that accompany emotional states in both humans and animals, while casting light on their origin and development. From a methodological point of view, his analysis builds for the most part on personal remarks and reports by other observers; in addition, Darwin makes extensive use of questionnaires, which even today represent the most common method for the analysis of expressions in the field of experimental psychology. From a theoretical and scientific standpoint, Darwin relies on three principles. The first is the 'principle of serviceable associated habits':

> Certain complex actions are of direct or indirect service under certain states of the mind, in order to relieve or gratify certain sensations, desires, etc.; and whenever the same state of mind is induced, however feebly, there is a tendency through the force of habit and association for the same movements to be performed, though they may not then be of the least use. Some actions ordinarily associated through habit with certain states of the mind may be partially repressed through the will, and in such cases the muscles which are least under the separate control of the will are the most liable still to act, causing movements which we recognise as expressive. In certain other cases the checking of one habitual movement requires other slight movements; and these are likewise expressive. (Darwin [1872]2009: 34)

The idea is that some expressions originally appeared as voluntary or reflex responses that were conducive to improving the survival and fitness of the individual, for example because they contributed to alleviating unpleasant feelings, to satisfying some given needs, or, in general, to optimizing a behavioural response. Over time, due to habit they have then rooted their way into behaviour, so that they appear exclusively by virtue of their association with the corresponding emotional states, regardless of whether or not they are of any use in those specific circumstances. A particularly telling example concerns an incident that happened to Darwin himself while he was observing a puff adder at the zoo: he approached the glass pane separating him from the snake, determined to avoid any reaction and to stay still during the attack; and yet, as soon as the snake attacked, he found himself jerking backwards. According to Darwin, the uncontrollable jolt that we perceive when facing a sudden threat comes from the acquisition of the habit of moving away from the danger as quickly as possible; this behaviour is often associated with the tendency to close our eyelids, since the eyes are particularly sensitive and vulnerable and need to be protected, and is always accompanied by an act of inhalation, through which the organism should prepare for a possible effort. Association and habit thus explain, for example, why we tend to close our eyes and to look away when presented with even just the thought of something disturbing or disgusting; they explain why the typical facial expression of an angry man, who lifts his lips so that his teeth are visible, suggests that he intends to attack by biting, even when he has no intention of starting a fight nor of engaging in aggressive behaviour. Darwin suggests an example related to animals that will be familiar to anyone who has ever had a cat: when a cat feels safe and lies comfortably on a warm, soft surface, it will often repeat the gestures it made when it used to exert a gentle pressure with its front paws on its mother's teats to stimulate the secretion of milk. Today we know that habitual behaviour is not transmitted as a hereditary feature, but Darwin was inclined to explain the persistence of automatic and no longer useful reactions on the basis of Lamarck's theory of the inheritance of acquired characteristics. Sometimes, however, he explicitly appealed to the principle of natural selection, showing how it provides a convincing justification for the principle of serviceable associated habits:

> reflex actions are in all probability liable to slight variations, as are all corporeal structures and instincts; and any variations which were beneficial and of sufficient importance would tend to be preserved and inherited. Thus reflex actions, when once gained for one purpose, might afterwards be modified independently of the will or habit, so as to serve for some distinct purpose. Such cases would be parallel with those which, as we have every reason to believe, have occurred with many instincts; for although some instincts have been developed simply through long-continued and inherited habit, other highly complex ones have been developed through the preservation of variations of pre-existing instincts – that is, through Natural Selection. (Darwin [1872]2009: 47)

Darwin's second principle, the so-called 'principle of antithesis', concerns those expressions that seem hardly useful, even for our ancestors, and whose origin can instead be explained by seeing them as antithetical to the expressions associated with the opposite emotional states:

> Certain states of the mind lead to certain habitual actions, which are of service, as under our first principle. Now when a directly opposite state of mind is induced, there is a strong and involuntary tendency to the performance of movements of a directly opposite nature, though these are of no use; and such movements are in some cases highly expressive. (Darwin [1872]2009: 34)

For example, the behaviour of a dog that spots a stranger and approaches him with hostility is intelligible if considered in relation to its intention to prepare for an attack: with its tail stiff and straight up, upright hair and firm gait, the dog starts growling while showing its canines and folding its ears back. When the dog comes close enough to recognize the stranger as its owner, its movements change radically, and express, according to Darwin, a diametrically opposed bodily attitude: the animal lowers and relaxes its tail, and ceases to growl and to clench its lips; its hair becomes softer and its ears are relaxed; this also changes the shape of its eyes, which appear more extended to the sides. An angry cat will crouch and stretch its body while swinging its tail; if engaged in predatory activity, it will fold its ears back and may even growl. These types of behaviour are apt to scare the enemy and to prepare for the attack. When, however, the cat is in the opposite emotional state, that is to say, when it feels safe and wishes to display the bond it enjoys with its owner, it will straighten its legs and tail while arching its back, and will start purring instead of growling. Darwin observed that, in this second scenario, the animal's posture and behaviour are of no obvious use. He thus concluded that they are performed by antithesis with respect to the characteristic features of the opposite affective state.

Finally, with the 'principle of the direct action of the nervous system' Darwin accounted for the role of the autonomic nervous system in regulating affective states:

> When the sensorium is strongly excited, nerve-force is generated in excess, and is transmitted in certain definite directions, depending on the connection of the nerve-cells, and partly on habit: or the supply of nerve-force may, as it appears, be interrupted. Effects are thus produced which we recognise as expressive. (Darwin [1872]2009: 34)

An interesting example, which shows that Darwin was aware of the bi-directional interactions between the autonomic nervous system and the brain, concerns cardiac activity:

> when the mind is strongly excited, we might expect that it would instantly affect in a direct manner the heart; and this is universally acknowledged and felt to be the case. . . . When the heart is affected it reacts on the brain; and the state of the brain again reacts through the pneumo-gastric nerve on the heart; so that under any excitement there will be much mutual action and reaction between these, the two most important organs of the body. (Darwin [1872]2009: 71–2)

Darwin's third principle explains, among other things, why we blush when we are ashamed, why we shiver when we are excited and why fear gives us goose pimples.

In short, the first principle holds that some expressions stem from responses that were originally conducive to maximizing the individual's success in the environmental circumstances that elicited the corresponding emotions. Other types of expressions and behaviour, by contrast, seem to be of no particular use: their origin is illustrated by the second principle, according to which they emerged by antithesis, that is, as elements associated with emotions that are the opposite of those that generate the expressions and movements illustrated by the first principle. Finally, with the third principle Darwin accounted for the (equally expressive) movements that are triggered by the activity of the autonomic nervous system.

The fundamental contribution of Darwin's research consisted first and foremost in providing a naturalistic explanation for behaviour, including human behaviour. As shown by the presence of evolutionary and universalist approaches in contemporary psychology, even today many of the ideas contained in *The Expression of the Emotions in*

Man and Animals continue to spark analysis and debate. Darwin's universalist intuition was crucial to the idea of the unity of mankind: 'I have endeavoured to show in considerable detail that all the chief expressions exhibited by man are the same throughout the world. This fact is interesting, as it affords a new argument in favour of the several races being descended from a single parent-stock' (Darwin [1872]2009: 355). Darwin made use of questionnaires and accounts of other observers to compare the manifestation of facial expressions of individuals from different and mutually isolated cultures.[5] 'It follows from the information thus acquired', he concluded, 'that the same state of mind is expressed throughout the world with remarkable uniformity; and this fact is in itself interesting, as evidence of the close similarity in bodily structure and mental disposition of all the races of mankind' (Darwin [1872]2009: 24).[6] At the same time, Darwin made a distinction between physical 'expressions' of emotions from signs and 'gestures', thus reconciling the universality of the former with the cultural variability of the latter:

> it seemed to me highly important to ascertain whether the same expressions and gestures prevail, as has often been asserted, without much evidence, with all the races of mankind, especially with those who have associated but little with Europeans. Whenever the same movements of the features or body express the same emotions in several distinct races of man, we may infer with much probability, that such expressions are true ones, that is, are innate or instinctive. Conventional expressions or gestures, acquired by the individual during early life, would probably have differed in the different races, in the same manner as do their languages. (Darwin [1872]2009: 22)[7]

Other interesting aspects emerge from Darwin's observations on the relationship between emotions, expressions and actions. First, thanks

to the principle of serviceable associated habits, Darwin identifies
a constitutive link between expressions and actions: the former did
not come about as external and visible signs of inner states (which is
something they became secondarily), but as behavioural responses, or
modes of action. We also have indirect proof of this, Darwin observes,
if we consider emotions such as envy or jealousy, whose outcome in
terms of action is not immediate: it is not accidental that there are no
distinctive expressions of these states of mind. Moreover, within the
framework of the principle of the direct action of the nervous system,
Darwin analysed the specific autonomic alterations of each emotion
and proposed an explanation based on the type of actions that these
prepare us to perform, in the light of the assumption that such actions
have proved useful in terms of adaptation. For example, pain is
associated with an attempt to escape from the stimulus that causes it –
hence the instinct, when one is injured, to shake the part of the body
that hurts as if this could help shake off the pain. Darwin concludes
that 'a habit of exerting with the utmost force all the muscles will have
been established, whenever great suffering is experienced' (Darwin
[1872]2009: 75). This analysis reveals a substantive connection
between emotion and what contemporary psychologists call 'action
tendencies':

> animals of all kinds, and their progenitors before them, when
> attacked or threatened by an enemy, have exerted their utmost
> powers in fighting and defending themselves. *Unless an animal
> does thus act, or has the intention, or at least the desire, to attack its
> enemy, it cannot properly be said to be enraged.* An inherited habit
> of muscular exertion will thus have been gained in association with
> rage; and this will directly and indirectly affect various organs, in
> nearly the same manner as does great bodily suffering. (Darwin
> [1872]2009: 78; emphasis added)[8]

In Darwin's view, there is a constitutive link also between emotion and expression:

> Most of our emotions are so closely connected with their expression that they hardly exist if the body remains passive – the nature of the expression depending in chief part on the nature of the actions which have been habitually performed under this particular state of mind. A man, for instance, may know that his life is in extremest peril, and may strongly desire to save it; yet as Louis XVI said when surrounded by a fierce mob, 'Am I afraid? Feel my pulse'. So a man may intensely hate another, *but until his bodily frame is affected* he cannot be said to be enraged. (Darwin [1872]2009: 234; emphasis added)[9]

Darwin analysed various implications of this deep-seated relation, such as the fact that emotional states tend to intensify when one gives way to them without trying to control their physical manifestations, while they tend to weaken when one makes an effort to keep those manifestations at bay:

> The free expression by outward signs of an emotion intensifies it. On the other hand, the repression, as far as this is possible, of all outward signs softens our emotions. He who gives way to violent gestures will increase his rage; he who does not control the signs of fear will experience fear in a greater degree; and he who remains passive when overwhelmed with grief loses his best chance of recovering elasticity of mind. These results follow partly from the intimate relation which exists between almost all the emotions and their outward manifestations; and partly from the direct influence of exertion on the heart, and consequently on the brain. Even the simulation of an emotion tends to arouse it in our minds. (Darwin [1872]2009: 359–60)[10]

These observations lend plausibility to the view that Darwin was inclined to regard emotion, expression and action not as distinct parts or components of the affective state, but rather as aspects of the same unity of experience.

Evolutionism

Many of Darwin's observations are still setting the agenda of contemporary research on emotions. Indeed, the very theoretical foundation of emotion studies in evolutionary psychology rests on the idea that certain types of behaviour and bodily changes originally appeared as responses functional to the fitness of the organism in specific environmental situations, and that they have been selected and preserved up to now although in the meantime they have become essentially useless.

Psychologist Leda Cosmides and anthropologist John Tooby, co-directors of the Center for Evolutionary Psychology at the University of California Santa Barbara, interpret the mind as a complex system of specialized programmes for solving different adaptation-related problems that have emerged throughout the evolutionary history of mankind (e.g. the need to find food and choose a partner, sleep management and defence against predators). Each of these programmes sets in as a response to specific environmental signals. Such programmes need coordination, and this, in turn, represents an adaptive challenge: the physiological and behavioural states required for sleep, for example, are incompatible with those required by the activation of the programme of escaping from a predator, and the simultaneous activation of two different programmes would generate a functional conflict that could be detrimental to survival. Cosmides and Tooby view emotions as superordinate mechanisms geared to manage specific programmes and selected to harmonize them. Each emotion represents an evolutionary response to a particular recurrent scenario within the 'Environment of Evolutionary Adaptedness',[11] and has the function of orchestrating multiple activities, such as perception, attention, assessment of probabilities and risks, memory, learning, physiological reactions such as the regulation of the heartbeat and of the endocrine system, actions, body movements, reflexes and so on. The activation of the fear programme, for example, produces changes in terms of perceptual focus (e.g. hearing becomes more acute), attention (e.g. the individual focuses on finding a place from which it can hear and see better), prioritization (e.g. the individual no longer feels hungry), mnemonic retrieval of information (e.g. the individual remembers a recent encounter with its adversaries and wonders whether they looked at it furtively), communicative processes (e.g. the individual shouts for help or remains motionless), physiological states (e.g. adrenaline spikes, heartbeat accelerates – or decelerates, if it is safer to remain still), as well as behaviour (e.g. the individual hides, runs away or remains motionless). According to Cosmides and Tooby, it is this sort of activation that defines the emotion of fear, regardless of whether the emotion is actually perceived as a matter of subjective experience.

Analysing emotions as adaptive responses means identifying a complex set of environmental properties and characteristics of the organism. First, one needs to recognize a recurrent situation, that is a statistical complex of co-variant elements. These may include being in a depleted nutritional state, being attacked by a predator, having few friends and allies, being ill, having achieved public success within the community and so on. It is on this basis that the adaptive challenge plays out, insofar as it becomes necessary to identify the most appropriate physical and behavioural states to tackle a problem or to exploit an opportunity. This is made possible by a proprioceptive and perceptual verification of well-defined signals (such as hypoglycaemia as an indication of malnutrition, an unfamiliar silhouette approaching rapidly as an indication of an attack by a predator, or social isolation as an indication of scarcity of friends and allies), so that if any of these signals are detected, a functionally suitable 'emotion program' is triggered. This leads to the activation of an organized mode of operation, which may in turn require triggering further emotion programmes. For example, in ancestral times a male with a sexually unfaithful partner risked losing power and social esteem, and was more likely to be attacked by competitors, even in other areas of his personal life, and this may explain the simultaneous occurrence of jealousy, anger and shame.

Within the framework of an emotional mode of operation, one's interactions with the environment are heavily influenced by specific perceptual and evaluative tendencies, which predispose the individual to interpret the context according to the expectations determined by the emotion programmes that have been triggered. The situational elements that appear relevant depend on the perspective suggested by the emotion programme: fear urges the individual to focus on the distinction between what is safe and what is not, while anger emphasizes the importance of aspects related to responsibility, guilt, and punishment. Emotional states have an impact on goals and priorities, as well as on the ability to retrieve information mnemonically; they steer one's focus, they alter physiological states, they make it easier or more difficult to perform certain tasks based on whether these are considered more or less useful (so that, for instance, it is easier to hit an enemy when one is angry than when one is scared). Overall, then, emotional states govern action and behaviour. In this sense, according to Cosmides and Tooby an emotion does not come down to any of its effects (whether these are physiological, cognitive or behavioural), but rather unfolds across the entire bodily and cognitive structure of the organism.

Universalism

Another key contribution to contemporary research provided by Darwin's theory lies in the following statement, which appears in the final chapter of *The Expression of the Emotions in Man and Animals*: 'I have endeavoured to show in considerable detail that all the chief expressions exhibited by man are the same throughout the world' (Darwin [1872]2009: 355). As Darwin saw it, the fact that emotions are linked to universal physical manifestations is a crucial piece of evidence in support of the view that human beings belong to the same species, and that emotions, along with their expressions, depend on innate biological instincts. In order to substantiate this claim, Darwin relied on methods that are still commonly used in contemporary psychology to investigate facial expressions. With these methods, which are based on questionnaires, people of different age, gender and cultural backgrounds are shown pictures and illustrations of different facial expressions and asked to identify and name the emotions they recognize.[12]

Psychologist Paul Ekman, who has devoted his entire career to the question of the universality of facial expressions of emotions, built his 'Basic Emotion Theory' (BET) upon Darwin's discoveries concerning the innate nature of emotions and theorized in this context the existence of certain primitive emotions.[13] In 1971, with the publication of a study entitled 'Universals and Cultural Differences in Facial Expressions of Emotion', Ekman presented his own 'neurocultural theory', which reconciled the demonstration of the existence of universal facial expressions with the acknowledgement of the role played by social and cultural learning in selecting the conditions that prompt emotional reactions (i.e. the so-called 'elicitors'), as well as in the determination of the so-called 'display rules', that is the rules based on which expressions, as well as behavioural consequences, both verbal and physical, of the emotional experience, are inhibited or emphasized depending on their appropriateness to the context.[14] It was thanks to a series of experiments modelled after Darwin's method that Ekman and his colleagues identified in different facial expression a set of universal constants dependent on 'facial affective programs' that specify the link between an emotion and the corresponding activation of a coordinated set of facial muscles, which are activated by a certain type of evaluation of environmental stimuli (however culturally variable the selection and interpretation of these stimuli may be). For example, observers from five different cultural groups were shown thirty pictures of faces of Caucasian adults and children, both male and female, with expressions related to specific emotions. At the same time, participants in the experiment were given a list of six emotion terms, each of which had to be matched with one or more pictures. Similar experiments, which involved using pictures and short stories in the native language of participants, were carried out on subjects belonging to oral cultures, whose exposure to Western media was estimated to be minimal. Based also on experimental results of other researchers,[15] Ekman and his colleagues concluded that they had successfully isolated a basic set of universal facial expressions:

> We believe, then, that we have isolated and demonstrated the basic set of universal facial expressions of emotion. They are not a language which varies from one place to another; one need not be taught a totally new set of muscular movements and a totally new set of rules for interpreting facial behavior if one travels from one culture to another. While facial expressions of emotion will

often be culture-specific because of differences in elicitors, display rules, and consequences, there is also a pancultural set of facial expressions of emotion. (Ekman 1971: 277)

What exactly does this universality thesis amount to? In a paper published in 1994, James Russell identified four possible formulations: '(a) universality of facial movements: specific patterns of facial muscle movement occur in all human beings, (b) expressiveness of facial movements: certain facial patterns are manifestations of the same emotions in all human beings, (c) universality of attribution: observers everywhere attribute the same emotional meaning to those facial patterns . . ., and (d) correctness of attributions: observers are correct in the emotions they (consensually) attribute to those facial patterns' (Russell 1994: 106). According to Russell, these four propositions should be considered independently of each other, because in principle not all of them may be true. It may be the case, for instance, that while all human beings share the same facial expressions of emotions, certain cultures could be less capable of interpreting and associating them with specific emotions compared to other cultures. In his view, one of the first critical aspects of research on emotional expressions lies precisely in the fact that those propositions are conflated with each other.

But the main shortcomings highlighted by Russell, who focused on research projects conducted since 1969 to test the hypothesis of cross-cultural uniformity in how observers link emotions and expressions, have to do with the experimental methods that were used, as well as with the tendency to interpret the results in such a way as to discard equally plausible alternative explanations. First, Russell observes that a response to a given stimulus always depends on contextualizing it in a wider network of stimuli: for example, a neutral expression may denote happiness if the context suggests joy; a sad face may appear enraged in the presence of other faces expressing anger, and so on.[16] The idea at work here mirrors the assumption behind the so-called Kulešov effect, demonstrated by the Russian film director Lev Vladimirovič Kulešov with the so-called *Mozžuchin* experiment: the observer is provided with contextual clues that lead him to recognize, in the same facial expression, different emotions depending on the frame to which the image of the face is juxtaposed in the editing phase. Consequently, the interpretation of a facial expression can be heavily influenced by the way in which the experiment is conducted. Some of the studies reviewed by Russell were set up in such a way that observers were first shown the entire set of images, and only afterwards asked to assess each of them individually; in other cases, observers were asked to associate expressions with emotions only after looking at the pictures several times; in yet other cases, researchers never changed the order in which the images were shown, thereby underestimating once again the influence of associations and contrasts between the various stimuli.

Another major issue that undermines the validity of the results obtained is that participants were given not only pictures, but also a list of emotion terms to choose from (for instance, in the case of Ekman, *happy, sad, scared, angry, surprised* and *disgusted* or *contemptuous*). Russell argues that

> A forced-choice format clearly alerts the subject to the experimenter's expectation that the facial expression is to be interpreted in terms of emotion and even which emotions. . . . Subjects . . . were not allowed to give *frustration, seeing a friend, attending to something novel,* or some other situational interpretation to the face. They were not allowed to describe the face as part of an instrumental response – such as *threatening, staring,* or *avoiding.* They were not given the option of choosing

a more general emotional state, such as *unhappy, distressed,* or *aroused.* . . . forcing the observer to choose exactly one option treats the set of options as mutually exclusive, which they are not: Subjects place the same facial expression (or emotion of another or their own emotion) into more than one emotion category. (Russell 1994: 116)

In this respect, not even the experiments that allowed participants to freely choose the emotion to be associated with the relevant expression were free from shortcomings: for even this method is built around the task of selecting only one emotion for each expression, and hence based on the implicit assumption that there must be a one-to-one correlation between a given expression and its corresponding emotion. Finally, Russell considers the research conducted by Ekman and his colleagues on tribal, non-Westernized populations not exposed to mass communication. Even in this case, he concludes that the results convey little information about either spontaneous expressions or those that were not selected by the experimenters, and ultimately fail to pay sufficient attention to the influence that context exerts on the emotional interpretation of facial expressions.

Finally, Russell proposes several alternative interpretations of the data emerging from the studies he investigates. Each of them endorses the assumption that there is indeed a (minimal) degree of universality (see Russell 1995), although he develops this within a broader perspective. The idea is that the experimental evidence available can be explained by the assumption that universal expressions do not relate to discrete emotions, but are rather linked to transversal dimensions such as hedonic tone (pleasant–unpleasant) and arousal (activated–sleepy). Such a hypothesis would also explain why the data show a high rate of convergence on the recognition of happy expressions (with high scores both on the hedonic and on the arousal scales) and a statistically lower agreement when it comes to anger and disgust (which share a similar intensity of arousal and a negative hedonic tone). Another hypothesis, which is not incompatible with the first one, holds that the interpretation of expressions is primarily instrumental (e.g. a smile signals that one wishes to greet a friend), whereby the relevant emotion is inferred only in a second step (e.g. one who meets a friend is usually happy).

Basic Emotion Theory

According to Paul Ekman, the manifestation of specific and universal expressive signals provides the most compelling evidence of the existence of *basic emotions*, that is of biologically inherited affective programmes with particular features. First of all, each basic emotion corresponds not only to distinctive and universal expressive signals but also to specific physiological alterations and eliciting stimuli,[17] whereby the recognition of these features would also be conducive to telling different emotions apart. Moreover, basic emotions are shared by other primates as well; their onset is rapid, so much that they may even precede individual awareness and be independent of the individual's will; they are short-lived and episodic; they are triggered by a mechanism of stimulus evaluation that acts automatically and unconsciously, producing consistent patterns of expressive manifestations and activation of the autonomic nervous system. This last group of properties is useful to distinguish emotions from different affective states. By 'basic emotion' Ekman does not mean a single affective state, but rather a family of related affective states that share a common theme (and, consequently, similar eliciting stimuli and similar expressive manifestations). In his view, each family represents a discrete category whose members share a set of defining essential features, which are biologically determined and inherited.[18] Learning as well as social and cultural influences can produce variations on the theme, whose nature remains however phylogenetically determined. Initially, Ekman drew up a list of six basic emotions (happiness, sadness, anger, fear, disgust and surprise),[19] to which he later added many others (including amusement, contempt, embarrassment, excitement, guilt, pride, relief, satisfaction, wonder, ecstasy, sensory pleasures and shame), claiming that their status would soon be warranted by empirical findings (Ekman and Cordaro 2011).

The best-known version of BET is undoubtedly that of Paul Ekman, but there are also other variants, such as the differential theory formulated by Carroll Izard (another pupil of Silvan Tomkins) or neuroscientist Jaak Panksepp's Emotional Command Systems. Still, in all these views basic emotions are to be considered adaptive products of evolutionary pressure, and are therefore 'primary' in a biological rather than a conceptual sense. Izard draws a rather sharp distinction between basic emotions (which he prefers to term 'first-order emotions') and 'emotion schemas', which emerge from the interaction between affective states and complex cognitive activities (such as abstract thought, planning, analysis, evaluation, etc.). After the earliest stages of infantile development, and unless emergency or alarm situations occur, our daily experience is shaped by emotion schemata. At the same time, according to Izard, primary emotions involve only the most basic cognitive functions of sense perception, so as to trigger the appropriate behavioural reactions quickly, and often automatically. These are simple-structure phenomena, characterized by an early phylogenetic and ontogenetic onset, with regulatory and motivational functions of crucial importance for the survival and well-being of the organism (e.g. Izard 2007). For Izard primary emotions are interest, happiness, sadness, anger, disgust and fear (when they occur in the absence of complex cognitive activities), to which he attributes specific neural circuits, distinctive feelings and motivational components, as well as peculiar behaviour and expressions (e.g. Izard 2011). These elementary emotion units are a product of evolutionary pressure and lay the basis for emotional schemata, of which we are capable since early childhood: rudimentary emotional schemata are, according to Izard, already inherent in the association, made even by young children, of feelings of joy and interest with images of human faces (Izard 1978).

From a neuroscientific perspective, Panksepp analyses basic emotions (which he terms 'primary-process core affects') within the framework of the evolutionary stratification of different brain functions in charge of affective regulation: primary affective functions, which are instinctive; secondary affective functions, which are related to learning; and tertiary affective functions, which involve complex cognitive activities such as thought, and emerge from the interaction of neocortical structures with limbic and paralimbic structures. From an anatomical point of view, Panksepp's approach rests on the assumption that the human brain is the product of three different evolutionary steps and can consequently be divided into (a) a reptilian brain (located in the midbrain), (b) a paleo-mammalian brain (located in the subcortical regions and in the most ancient regions of the cortex, such as the insula), and (c) the neocortex, the most recent part, in charge of more sophisticated functions (such as language, abstract thought, etc.).[20] According to Panksepp, primary, secondary and tertiary affective functions correspond to these anatomical regions. The affective life of an adult is predominantly made up of secondary and tertiary processes, but there is no scientific evidence that the neocortex is capable of generating affective feelings without the involvement of the limbic and subcortical emotional effector systems. At the same time, through the artificial activation of subcortical regions of the brain it is possible to induce primary processes that can be traced back to basic affective systems, which for Panksepp are SEEKING, FEAR, RAGE, LUST, CARE, PANIC/GRIEF and PLAY, and which are shared by all mammals.[21] Secondary and tertiary affective processes derive from these primary activations, and so much so that, according to Panksepp, it may be useful on a heuristic level to group the former into families of shared functionalities and to reconstruct their precognitive relation with primary processes from a biochemical standpoint (for instance, if we suppose that the sense of guilt represents a cognitively complex processing of primary separation anxiety, we can assume that opioids, which significantly ease separation anxiety in animals, may inhibit the feeling of guilt in humans).

Unlike Ekman, who maintains that 'an emotion is either basic, or it is another affective phenomenon' (Ekman and Cordaro 2011: 365), both Izard and Panksepp endorse the idea that basic emotions are 'building blocks' of more complex emotions: as we have seen, Izard believes that 'first-order emotions' are the core elements of emotional schemata, while Panksepp holds that complex emotions derive from primary processes. If the phenomenon of emotions, both basic and complex, is unitary, then we need to identify the mechanisms by virtue of which primary processes become part, as constituents, of secondary and tertiary ones. Two main theories have been put forward in this regard, namely Plutchik's mechanism of blending and Damasio's one of cortical elicitation. Drawing on an idea advanced by William McDougall, in an article published in *American Scientist* in 2001 psychologist Robert Plutchik suggested conceptualizing emotions through an analogy with colours. He thus devised a wheel of emotions in which opposite emotions are placed at a distance of 180° from each other, based on a well-ordered arrangement of eight primary emotions (joy, acceptance, fear, surprise, sorrow, disgust, anger and expectancy) and their variants in terms of intensity. Just as a mixture of yellow and blue produces green, so, according to Plutchik, the combination of two primary emotions produces corresponding 'primary dyads': for example, the mixture of *joy* and *acceptance* produces the mixed emotion of *love*, while the mixture of *fear* and *surprise* produces *awe*. The *sense of guilt*, instead, would appear to be a *secondary dyad*, resulting from the combination of two non-contiguous emotions (i.e. *joy* and *fear*), while *shame* would instead be a *tertiary dyad* emerging from the mixture of primary emotions with three degrees of mutual distance (i.e. *fear* and *disgust*). The unification mechanism proposed by Plutchik is highly problematic, for it appears quite evident that from a phenomenological standpoint dyads do not come down to a simple combination of their elements. For example, the feelings of someone in love are qualitatively different from the feelings that accompany joy and acceptance, and so are the typical types of behaviour and expressive manifestations connected to love. The same certainly applies to the sense of guilt, shame and the other primary, secondary and tertiary constructions envisaged by Plutchik.

Antonio Damasio holds that primary emotions, which are innate, pre-organized and dependent on the circuits of the limbic system (and, in particular, of the amygdala), constitute the basic mechanism of secondary emotions, which arise after the acquisition of the capacity to establish systematic connections between primary emotions and their eliciting stimuli. The more complex nature of secondary emotions requires, according to Damasio, the intervention of the prefrontal cortex. The fear reaction that many animals exhibit automatically when they encounter a predator is an example of a primary emotion, which emerges from the most ancient and deepest areas of the brain. A secondary emotion, by contrast, is generated when this very same mechanism is activated cortically, that is following a cognitive assessment of the quality of the stimulus. By analysing circumscribed brain lesions, Damasio adds further evidence in support of the claim that the neural circuits controlling emotions serve specific functions: patients suffering from lesions of the prefrontal cortex are incapable of secondary emotional experience, while they keep processing primary emotions; patients with lesions of the limbic system, instead, present a more extensive impairment, which also involves primary emotions. Damasio's picture is consistent with Joseph LeDoux's hypothesis of a dual pathway (i.e. both thalamic and cortical) of fear elicitation (LeDoux 1996). LeDoux's model suggests that fear reactions can occur subcortically, thus bypassing the neocortex. This would mean that the intervention of the brain systems controlling the conscious processes of thought and reasoning would be superfluous to the elicitation of primary emotions, while they would only effect secondary, 'cognitive' emotions, characterized by a slower onset. Both Damasio and LeDoux rely on an interpretation of brain functioning that implies a neural separation between 'emotion' and 'cognition'. Contrary to this view, which is becoming increasingly controversial, there are now many alternative approaches that show how cognition and emotion intersect and overlap with each other, to such an extent that it may be appropriate to jettison the cognition–emotion divide altogether.

Alternatives and criticism
Biology or culture?

Constructionism

The central idea of BET, in all its variants, is that basic or primary emotions are innate, biologically inherited modules distinctively linked to physiological, expressive and behavioural reaction programmes, which are systematically interrelated. Consequently, BET theorists are committed to the view that all instances of a given emotion (such as *fear*) are similar to each other, since they are caused by the same affective programme, which can be identified, measured, and classified by virtue of its essential properties (such as expressive manifestations, physiological alterations, eliciting conditions and so on). Basic emotions would thus amount to biological entities independent of linguistic, social, cultural and conceptual influences.[1] Although still dominant in affective science, this view has attracted several lines of criticism, and is attacked with particular emphasis by scholars endorsing a constructionist approach.

Psychological constructionism rejects the thesis invoked by BET theorists according to which common-sense psychological categories such as *anger* or *fear* can be scientifically analysed as primary elements, and suggests instead that emotions are the result of the subjective, culturally, socially and linguistically inflected interpretation of psychologically simple affective alterations that take place on the valence and arousal scales. For constructionists, variability is an essential aspect of emotional experience, which any valid theory must properly take into account. For instance, in criticizing the thesis that neurophysiological response modules are systematically linked to common-sense categories, along with the thesis that basic emotions are psychological *primitives*, James Russell argues that

> There may be no one scientific model that applies to all cases of fear, and only to fear. . . . Gone is the assumption that all events called *emotion* or *fear* or *anger* can be accounted for in the same way. These concepts are not abandoned but are put in their proper place as folk rather than as scientific concepts, and their role limited to whatever role folk concepts actually play in emotion (and in perception of emotion in others). (Russell 2003: 146)

Constructionists thus set out to look for elementary constituents of emotions. These constituents are not specific to emotions but are rather domain-general factors (e.g. psychological, interoceptive or linguistic processes) whose combination brings about different emotions, just as different combinations of the same ingredients can produce different recipes. According to Russell, one of these ingredients is 'core affect', that is a 'neurophysiological state that is consciously accessible as a simple, nonreflective feeling that is an integral blend of hedonic (pleasure–displeasure) and arousal (sleepy–activated) values' (Russell 2003: 147). To put it more simply, *core affect* is a two-dimensional conscious *feeling*, in the sense that it varies on the horizontal valence scale (pleasure and displeasure: from the extreme of agony to that of ecstasy, through intermediate degrees of adaptation) and on the vertical scale of arousal (from sleep to drowsiness along different states of alertness and up to frenetic excitement). Core affect is a kind of evaluation of how we feel and of our energy level. It is a basic affective state which cannot be further broken down and whose existence does not depend on its being categorized, interpreted or traced back to a given cause. It is not about anything in particular (i.e. it has no intentional object), but it can be combined with additional components, such as a stimulus.

Against the background of our experience, we always perceive some kind of feeling, which means that core affect is always at play, while its variations can depend on many factors, both endogenous (e.g. hormonal activity, the activity of the immune system and so on) and, of course, exogenous: the stimuli coming from the environment are characterized by an 'affective quality' that interferes with core affect, thereby modifying it. The idea is that the perception of the affective quality of external stimuli is a constitutive part of our cognitive processes, and hence always present. In other words, any perception has an affective quality, which can cause a change in core affect. On the other hand, core affect will in turn interfere with the affective quality of the stimulus we perceive at a given moment: the same stimulus that in ordinary conditions would go almost unnoticed may be perceived as particularly unpleasant when we are tired or ill, while when we are in a good mood we are more likely to evaluate as pleasant or positively exciting the stimuli gathered from the environment (e.g. Petrolini and Viola 2020). Finally, a third primary process is what Russell calls 'attributed affect', that is the association of core affect with a perceived stimulus that we interpret as its cause. It is from the various combinations of these three elementary ingredients (core affect, perception of affective quality and attributed affect) that emotions can emerge.

An emotional episode thus includes various aspects. First there is an antecedent (i.e. an event or external stimulus) of which we perceive the affective quality. This first process produces a variation in our core affect, as this is associated with the antecedent, which in turn is identified as its cause. At the same time, the antecedent is assessed along with its implications, such as the impact it will have on future goals. Changes in core affect generate expressive reactions and physiological changes that prepare us to act instrumentally with respect to the antecedent, that is to behave in such a way as to reduce or maximize its effect, depending on whether it is considered a problem or an opportunity. Only when the state of mind is categorized from a meta-emotional point of view, that is classified as – say – an instance of *fear* or *anger*, do we come across what is commonly referred to by the notions of *fear* and *anger* – notions that BET instead construes as pointing to indivisible primary entities.

In contrast to BET, therefore, psychological constructionism rejects the view that emotions have specific biological markers. Rather, emotions are viewed as categories that include an infinite number of individual occurrences: they are the result of a subjective construction, that is of the association of an experiential process with a linguistic and cultural notion. Although the constructionist thesis is not backed by much experimental evidence, there is some research that supports this type of approach. For example, Lindquist, Barrett and colleagues have completed a study that challenges one of BET's core theses, namely the view that the ability to recognize the emotions of others by looking at facial expressions is innate, universal and pre-linguistic. To do so, they examined three patients suffering from a neurodegenerative disease called semantic dementia, which causes major deficits in the ability to understand the meaning of words. These patients were no longer able to recognize emotions using common-sense linguistic categories (such as *fear, anger, disgust* and so on), but they retained the ability to spontaneously perceive the valence (pleasant–unpleasant) of the affective state of which they were observing the expressions. This result was interpreted as supporting the hypothesis that emotion-related concepts help turn perceptions of valence into discrete emotion perceptions (Lindquist et al. 2014; but see Macoir et al. 2019). In a similar vein, Russell and Widen concluded from their observation of children between the ages of two and five that the ability to identify different emotions develops in conjunction with the acquisition of the corresponding common-sense categories: young children simply interpret others' facial expressions on the basis of the distinction between positive and negative affective states, and acquire the ability to make specific classifications only at a later stage (Widen and Russell 2008; Widen 2016).

At the same time, some constructionist criticisms of scientific findings that show a systematic correlation between specific patterns of nervous activation and certain so-called basic emotions are perhaps a little too harsh. In a 2006 paper, for example, Lisa Barrett stated that meta-analyses show that it is not possible to distinguish categories such as *anger*, *fear*, *sadness*, *happiness* and *disgust* in relation to their respective patterns of autonomic activity (Barrett 2006). In fact, the studies reviewed by Barrett identify, albeit cautiously, a certain degree of systematicity between the activation of specific areas of the nervous system and certain specific emotions.[2] In this sense, a non-dichotomic approach that seeks to reconcile the thesis of cultural variability with that of biological universality may turn out to be the most promising option.

There are three main variants of the constructionist approach to emotions: psychological constructionism (as in the version endorsed by Russell) suggests that emotions are phenomena constructed out of elementary psychological processes that produce affective meaning; social constructionism, instead, analyses the influence exerted by social roles and values on the construction of affective responses; finally, neuroconstructionism is concerned with the phenomenon of brain plasticity and with how our experience can lead to the formation of certain neural circuits. Lisa Feldman Barrett's conceptual act theory integrates all three variants of constructionism by appealing to the hypothesis, couched in terms of 'predictive coding', 'active inference' or 'belief propagation', that cognitive processes are not the result of a *reactive* activity of the brain in response to environmental stimuli, but rather the outcome of some *predictive* activity. On this view, the brain continuously generates hypotheses based on previous experience and tests them against external sensory data in a top–down fashion. The so-called top–down effects on sensory perception are backed by substantial empirical evidence. Consider, for example, how visual perception works: there are three types of cones in the retina, each of which has pigments that are sensitive to different wavelengths. The sensation of colour, however, is not formed in the retina but in the brain, and the operation performed by the brain is not just a matter of combining the signals coming from photoreceptors. Before the light stimulus can lead to the perception of the colour, several crucial steps have to take place (i.e. normalization, compensation, stabilization and regulation). At the same time, desires and expectations also interfere with the process through which a sensation is formed. For example, if the brain has reason to believe, on the basis of previous experience, that the object we are looking at should have a certain colour, then it is likely to make us see that colour even when this is in fact not present. An experiment conducted in 2006 by Hansen and colleagues provided a telling example of this phenomenon. Participants were shown a random series of coloured dots on a computer screen and asked to change the colour of the dots by pressing a button repeatedly until they became completely grey. This was not a particularly difficult task, and each participant was able to complete it. The experiment was then repeated a second time, with the difference however that the coloured dots on screen had been replaced with images of fruit. In this case too, participants were asked to press the button to change the colour of the fruit until it appeared grey. This time, however, they did not stop when the fruit became *objectively* grey: as they kept seeing traces of colour, they kept pressing the button so many times that the images eventually turned bluish (Hansen et al. 2006). Barrett suggests that the brain behaves in the same way when it interprets sensations from inside the body, such as breathing and heart rate, muscle tension and, in general, physiological states and their alterations. Interoceptive sensations, according to Barrett, have no psychological significance until they are classified by the brain based on past experience and information emerging from the specific context around the organism, thereby activating the relevant representational categories; insofar as these categories are emotional, the brain constructs an emotion (Barrett 2017a, b). Consequently, our ability to feel an emotion (and to perceive it in others) depends on the culturally and socially specific concepts we use to interpret stimuli and situations, identify their properties and associate them with linguistically determined categories such as *anger, fear, disgust, surprise* and so on. Thus, far from being innate modules, purportedly basic emotions constitute abstract categories that comprise specific occurrences, which are highly variable from a physiological, expressive and behavioural standpoint, and whose variability reflects different strategies of interaction with the relevant eliciting situations. The concepts we use to attribute meaning to eliciting stimuli derive from what we have learned both theoretically and through experience and observation, and are informed by the knowledge that emerges from the association of different concepts, as well as by previous associations of a given concept with specific interoceptive states. Whenever we resort to a common-sense category and compare past experiences with current ones, we contribute to extending the range of instances that this category encompasses. Our vocabulary also plays an important role in the process of conceptualization, since each emotion-specific term is associated with a series of situational, behavioural and phenomenological features that selectively direct our attention to the stimuli surrounding us. In conclusion, according to Barrett,

> An emotion is your brain's creation of what your bodily sensations mean, in relation to what is going on around you in the world. . . . In every waking moment, your brain uses past experience, organised as concepts, to guide your actions and give your sensations meaning. . . . When the concepts involved are emotion concepts, your brain constructs instances of emotion. . . . Emotions are not . . . reactions to the world. You are not a passive receiver of sensory input but an active constructor of your emotions. From sensory input and past experience, your brain constructs meaning and prescribes action. (Barrett 2017b: 30–1)

Cognition-arousal theory

Barrett's approach shows significant analogies with the theory that Stanley Schachter and Jerome Singer proposed in the early 1960s with the publication of the experimental study entitled 'Cognitive, Social, and Psychological Determinants of Emotional State'.[3] The core idea of this study is that the body's contribution to emotional experience is undifferentiated, in a way that makes it impossible to tell emotions apart on the basis of patterns of activation of the autonomic nervous system.[4] This, in turn, led the authors to embrace the hypothesis that the same state of physiological alteration can be justified in the light of different explanations, depending on the information that an individual identifies as relevant in a given context. Thus, the assumption that there is a sharp distinction between physiological and cognitive activity emerges clearly in a perspective that confines the role of the body to sheer activation processes, which acquire emotional meaning only to the extent that they are interpreted 'cognitively'.

As regards the experimental part of their work, Schachter and Singer drew on the research of Spanish physician Gregorio Marañon on the physiological and psychological effects of adrenaline injections. In 1924, Marañon injected 210 patients with a dose of adrenaline and then asked them to reflect introspectively. A total of 71 per cent of the patients simply described their physical symptoms, while the remaining 29 per cent qualified their descriptions by analogy with specific emotional states (using for instance expressions such as 'I feel *as if* I were scared'). Schachter and Singer note that since Marañon's patients knew that they had received an adrenaline injection, and were probably also aware at least of its general effects on the body, such as the increase in blood pressure and heart rate, they had a proper explanation of their feelings ready to hand. Schachter and Singer thus decided to repeat the experiment, which was, however, this time set up with the purpose of observing what happens when one experiences a major physiological alteration without having any immediate and explicit information about its causes. To this end, they informed participants that the purpose of the experiment was to test the effects that a vitamin supplement named Suproxin has on vision. Participants were divided into two groups: the first group received an injection of epinephrine, and the second group an injection of saline solution. Participants who received epinephrine were in turn divided into three subgroups: the members of the first subgroup were informed that the injection can cause side effects such as tremor and tachycardia (which are the real effects of epinephrine), while those of the second group were misinformed and told that side effects included itching and headache; finally, the members of the third group were given no information at all. At this point, an actor disguised as a regular participant joined the experiment and behaved in such a way as to elicit alternatively euphoria and irritation; at the end of the experiment, participants were asked to fill out a questionnaire with several questions concerning their state of mind. Those who received an injection of saline solution did not report any significant emotional experience; on the other hand, among the subjects who received a dose of epinephrine, those who were informed about possible side effects were less susceptible to the emotional manipulation performed by the actor.

According to Schachter and Singer, these results show two things: first, that no emotional episode can be experienced in the absence of physiological alteration; second, that the same state of physiological alteration can be explained by an appeal to radically different emotional states, such as euphoria and anger. In this respect, however, it is worth noting that heart rate is the only physiological parameter actually measured in the study conducted by Schachter and Singer, who never contemplated the possibility that the autonomic activity of participants might undergo other alterations specific to euphoria and anger.[5] In any event, the thesis that in the absence of an immediate and convincing explanation for a given state of physiological alteration there is a tendency to work out a subjective justification for it on the basis of the information available in a given context is undoubtedly akin to the constructionist notion of 'situated conceptualization'. At the same time, the idea that emotions are the upshot of the way in which we represent certain bodily states has strong similarities, as Barrett herself points out, to the constructionist approach, which regards emotions as cultural, social and linguistic products devoid of specific biological markers (Barrett 2017b: 33–4).[6]

Debate I
The emotions of others

With regard to the bodily manifestations of emotions, a crucial issue concerns the question of how they relate to the corresponding mental states. Is this a causal relation, such that what is visible (e.g. tears) is nothing but the external effect of a previous mental event that remains invisible (e.g. sorrow)? Or is it perhaps the case, as Charles Darwin seemed to suggest, that expressions and emotions are inextricably intertwined so as to form an indivisible unity? So far, we have been discussing states of mind and expressive behaviour mainly from the point of view of the individual. If, however, we start considering the social interactions around which our everyday life revolves, a core question comes to the fore: How can we explain our ability to understand the feelings of others? More specifically: Do expressions and behaviour owe their meaning to the relationship they exhibit with their corresponding mental states, or are they rather imbued with some intrinsic psychological meaning?

Indeed, it is by looking at how philosophers and psychologists answer this question that we can map out the main different views on social cognition and theory of mind.[1] On the one hand, some believe that in order to explain the transition from the observation of certain changes in observable symptoms (e.g. blushing), bodily movements and posture (e.g. shoulder protraction) and facial expressions (e.g. staring look and tight lips) to the attribution of a specific mental state (e.g. anger) one needs to postulate an intermediate step, namely a process that, by either inference or simulation, ascribes psychological meaning to pieces of information that carry no meaning per se. This category encompasses several proposals that fall within the scope of so-called 'theory theory' as well as of 'simulation theory'. According to theory theory, our understanding of others is based on adopting a theoretical attitude, that is on inferring the best explanation from the way in which common-sense psychology usually interprets the relationship between mental states and behaviour.[2] Some, including Alison Gopnik and Andrew Meltzoff, believe that the ability to understand what others think and feel emerges through an abstract learning process that begins in early childhood: children collect evidence and test hypotheses as if they were scientists in a laboratory, thus learning to generalize relations of cause and effect between beliefs, expressions, desires, affects and actions (Gopnik and Meltzoff 1997, 2013). Learning about the mind, which is shaped by the innate assumption of similarity between one's own mental states and those of others (the 'like-me hypothesis')[3], is therefore explained by analogy with theory change in science: within the general framework of the 'like-me hypothesis', infants accumulate evidence, test suppositions, and revise concepts and theories. Others, such as Alan Leslie and Simon Baron-Cohen, argue in favour of the existence of innate modules that allow, and at the same time constrain, the development of the ability to 'mentalize' (Leslie 1994; Baron-Cohen 1995). As opposed to Gopnik and Meltzoff's 'framework principle' (Gopnik and Meltzoff 2013: 21), the innate structures that modularity theories posit are not defeasible. Therefore, experience and the acquisition of evidence play a minor role, and a limited set of changes and variations is actually possible. In both cases, however, the basic idea is that the attribution of thoughts and emotions to others occurs theoretically and inferentially: since it is impossible to access the thoughts, emotions and, in general, the mental states of others through direct experience,[4] we can only postulate their existence theoretically, and hence indirectly.[5]

According to simulation theory, on the other hand, we understand others because we simulate their states of mind, modelling their experience after our own. We explicitly resort to this process when we put ourselves in the other's shoes, as it were: in cases of this kind, we ascribe to ourselves fictitious states of mind, we analyse introspectively their implications and potential consequences, and eventually we project onto the other the conclusions we have reached (Gordon 1986; Goldman 1989). The 'implicit' variant of this theory, which was first formulated by Gallese and Goldman in 1998, assumes instead that simulation occurs at the level of the subpersonal activation of mirror neurons. Mirror neurons were discovered in the premotor cortex of macaques in the early 1990s (Rizzolatti et al. 1996; Gallese et al. 1996), and their existence in humans was confirmed shortly after (Fadiga et al. 1995). They are called 'mirror neurons' because they fire both when the subject performs a certain action and when he or she observes another performing it:

> Whenever we are looking at someone performing an action, beside the activation of various visual areas, there is a concurrent activation of the motor circuits that are recruited when we ourselves perform that action. Although we do not overtly reproduce the observed action, nevertheless our motor system becomes active *as if* we were executing that very same action that we are observing. To spell it out in different words, action observation implies *action simulation*. . . . In other words, when we observe actions performed by other individuals our motor system 'resonates' along with that of the observed agent. (Gallese 2001: 37–8)

The discovery of this process of motor resonance, which takes place in a spontaneous, pre-reflective and non-inferential way, led to the hypothesis that the attribution of mental states to others depends precisely on the mirroring mechanism made possible by mirror neurons, which induces a process of implicit simulation in the observer. The relationship between mirroring and mindreading can be interpreted in different ways: Vittorio Gallese, for instance, believes that the activation of the mirroring system is constitutive of the ability to attribute mental states to others (Gallese 2005, 2007). Alvin Goldman maintains instead that the additional, specific processes that are typical of mindreading are induced by 'low-level' simulation processes (Goldman 2006). In any event, simulation theory assumes that our access to the mind of others is always and necessarily mediated by our own mind, which we use as a model. If this is the case, then the thorniest question that this theory needs to address is whether it is at all possible to understand others, since any attempt at understanding others would always be tantamount to projecting ourselves onto them.

Although contemporary debate features many different variants of both views, as well as hybrid versions that draw equally on both approaches, there is a central assumption upon which all versions of theory theory and of simulation theory (whether explicit and implicit) seem to converge, namely the idea that the mind is something private and that nobody has direct knowledge of other people's mind, which can only be accessed by inference and analogy. A very different perspective has its roots in twentieth-century philosophy, especially in classical phenomenology and in the second Wittgenstein. Its more recent formulations are variously referred to as the 'direct-perception model' (e.g. Krueger and Overgaard 2012), the 'phenomenological proposal' (e.g. Zahavi 2011), or 'direct social perception' (in the context of Shaun Gallagher's interaction theory: e.g. Gallagher 2020). These tend to be pluralistic approaches, which acknowledge that our understanding of others is made possible by a variety of different processes (including, in certain situations, those described by theory theory and by simulation theory), but at the same time maintain that direct perception is one central dimension of our social experience. The basic idea is that the mind of others is not private and inaccessible, as intentions and dispositions manifest themselves at least partly in behaviour as well as in face and body movements. Inference or simulation may be necessary tools in hard-to-decipher situations, but ordinary interactions among human beings are informed by the immediate perception of the subjectivity and mental states of others, contextualized in specific physical and social situations. From this perspective, understanding the emotions of others does not entail a process of simulation and imaginative projection, nor does it involve an inferential transition from visible physical manifestations to an invisible inner state, but is rather a matter of direct perception of aspects such as actions, expressions and behaviour, which constitute and contextualize emotional experience.[6] This is the rationale behind what Max Scheler claims in *Essence and Forms of Sympathy*:

> that experiences occur there [in the other person] is given for us in expressive phenomena – . . . not by inference, but directly, as a sort of primary 'perception'. It is *in* the blush that we perceive shame, *in* the laughter joy. (Scheler [1923] 1973: 21)[7]

The same idea is expressed by Wittgenstein in the following terms: 'Do you look into yourself in order to recognize the fury in his face? . . . . "We see emotion". – As opposed to what? – We do not see facial contortions and make inferences from them (like a doctor framing a diagnosis) to joy, grief, boredom. We describe a face immediately as sad, radiant, bored, even when we are unable to give any other description of the features' (Wittgenstein [1967] 2007: 220, 225). Wittgenstein's notion of 'family resemblances' has paved the way for the idea that emotions are modules characterized by a certain number of typical though not necessary features. These features, which include physiological alterations, the inclination to act in a certain way, bodily manifestations (posture, facial expressions, tone of voice, etc.), subjective feelings, doxastic aspects, judgements of value and intentional objects, are constitutive of each emotion in a non-essentialist sense: each of them represents an aspect that, in combination with others, is sufficient though not necessary for an emotion to occur (Newen, Welpinghus and Juckel 2015). Recognizing an emotion, then, means perceiving a set of factors that vary individually and yet are significant insofar as they are coordinated within the framework of a coherent module that also includes salient contextual aspects.

The idea that expressions and behaviour are imbued with intrinsic psychological meaning is backed by extensive experimental evidence. Several studies focusing on the consequences of the manipulation of expressive behaviour in terms of subjective phenomenology have shown that mental states and corresponding physical manifestations are constitutively interdependent, and do not follow a pattern of cause and effect (Laird 2007). According to the hypothesis of facial feedback, facial expressions contribute to producing corresponding emotional feelings (e.g. Duclos et al. 1989; Wilcox and Laird 2000; Duclos and Laird 2001), or else to intensifying or inhibiting them (e.g. Gross 1998; Gross and Levenson 1993, 1997; Davis et al. 2010), as well as to facilitating the processing of emotion-related information (e.g. Niedenthal et al. 2001; Niedenthal 2007; Havas et al. 2010; Neal and Chartrand 2011). The same applies to body posture (e.g. Riskind 1983, 1984; Duclos et al. 1989; Stepper and Strack 1993; Flack, Lair and Cavallaro 1999). Thus, subjects who are given an electric shock tend to report a higher pain level when they are asked to emphasize their feelings with facial expressions, and a lower one when they are asked to inhibit their expressions (Lanzetta, Cartwright-Smith and

Eleck 1976). The emotions felt when watching a film are experienced less intensively by subjects who received Botox injections and more intensively by those who received Restylane injections (which, unlike Botox, does not paralyse facial muscles; Davis et al. 2010), while the same comic strip is considered more or less funny depending on the way in which the subjects reading it are asked to hold a pen between their teeth (i.e. crosswise to simulate a smile, or perpendicularly to simulate a grumpy expression; Strack, Martin and Stepper 1988). If gestures and expressions play such a major role in shaping subjective emotional experience, we must conclude that inner state and somatic manifestation are not separate dimensions of emotion, and should not be conceptualized independently of one another.

Bodily feedback is a key factor relied upon by researchers who believe that our ability to recognize the emotions of others is rooted in the phenomenon of emotional contagion, which is in turn made possible by our innate and spontaneous tendency to imitate the expressions of others. Extensive experimental evidence confirms that in face-to-face interaction we tend to automatically and spontaneously replicate the expressive behaviour of others (e.g. Chartrand and Bargh 1999; Dimberg and Thunberg 1998; Dimberg, Thunberg and Elmehed 2000; Cannon, Hayes and Tipper 2009). Facial electromyography has revealed that the observation of images of happy faces is associated with an increased activity from the zygomatic major muscle region, whereas the exposure to angry expressions induces a more intense contraction of the corrugator supercilii muscle (Dimberg 1982); the same happens when images of faces are shown using the backward-masking technique so as to prevent conscious perception in the observer (Dimberg, Thunberg and Elmehed 2000; Sonnby-Borgström 2002), and when observers are explicitly instructed not to change their facial mimicry while they look at the images (Dimberg, Thunberg and Grunedal 2002). Finally, several neuroimaging studies show that the brain areas involved when we feel an emotion are activated also when we observe the same emotion experienced by someone else (e.g. Wicker et al. 2003; Avenanti et al. 2005; Wicker et al. 2003; Avenanti et al. 2005; Botvinick et al. 2005; Jackson, Meltzoff and Decety 2005; van der Gaag, Minderaa and Keysers 2007). The hypothesis according to which mindreading is made possible by imitation, understood as the cause of emotional contagion, holds that by replicating in our faces and bodies the expressive manifestations of the emotions of others we end up feeling the same emotions by virtue of a feedback mechanism; by experiencing them first-hand we can understand and classify them, and eventually attribute them to others (e.g. Hatfield, Cacioppo and Rapson 1994; Hatfield, Rapson and Le Yen-Chi 2009). Although it has gained much currency in contemporary debate,[8] the link between emotional convergence and mindreading is not a novel idea. Indeed, one of the most powerful renditions of this intuition dates back to the mid-seventeenth century, as expressed in Cyrano de Bergerac's *Histoire comique des états et empires du soleil*:

> Walking about there, I met with a very venerable old Man, who observed that famous conflict, with no less curiosity than my self. He made me a sign to draw nigh, I obeyed, and we sat down by one another.
>
> I had a design to have asked him the motive, that had brought him into that Country, but he stopt my Mouth with these words; Well then, you shall know the motive, that brought me into this Country. And thereupon he gave me a full account of all the particulars of his Voyage. I leave it to you to judge, in what amazement I was. In the mean while, to increase my consternation, as I was boyling with desire to ask him, what Spirit revealed my thoughts to him: No, no, cryed he, it's no Spirit that reveals your thoughts to me –

This new hit of Divination, made me observe him with greater attention than before, and I perceived that he acted my Carriage, my Gestures and Looks, that he postured all his Members, and shaped all the parts of his Countenance, according to the pattern of mine; in a word, my Shadow in relief could not have represented me better. I see, said he, you are in pain to know why I counterfeit you, and I am willing to tell you. Know then, that to the end I might know your inside, I disposed all the parts of my Body, into the same Order I saw yours in; for being in all parts situated like you, by that disposition of matter, I excite in my self the same thought, that the same disposition of matter raises in you. (Cyrano de Bergerac [1657-1162] 1886: 224–5; trans. Lovell)[9]

In Cyrano's narrative, Tommaso Campanella understands the thoughts of the protagonist by imitating his posture and movements, but it is not clear whether and to what extent this brings about an emotional convergence between them.[10] The contemporary hypothesis, on the other hand, is very explicit about the need to experience the emotions of the other in order to recognize them, and for this very reason turns out to be rather problematic on a phenomenological level. As a general rule, we react to the emotions of others, for instance by becoming scared if we see an angry face, or by smiling when smiled at. As we react, we may experience an emotion of the same kind as the one we are responding to, such as when we feel sad because a loved one is sad. Here, however, our experience and our emotions remain distinct from the experience and the emotions of the other. Of course, we may share the same emotion as another person, but what this really means is that we share the object to which the emotion is directed (as when two friends enjoy the same film or laugh at the same joke), and not the emotion itself. Sharing emotions can be a crucial aspect of one's emotional experience, and can enable emotions that would have otherwise never occurred. Again, though, while we may share an emotion *with* another person, it is never the case that we share the actual emotion *of* the other person.

The classical, simulationist view of the phenomenon of facial mimicry is not the only possible approach. The experimental data available on how our bodies respond to the bodies of others during face-to-face interactions can also be accounted for by an alternative model, which goes under the heading of 'emotion mimicry in context'. According to Ursula Hess and Agneta Fischer, the results obtained from the study of facial mimicry do not show a tendency to imitate specific emotions, but rather a tendency to respond with expressions that are consistent with the general affective quality of the expression observed. Moreover, the context in which interactions take place is a constitutive aspect of the stimuli to which we react, whereas the available data on facial mimicry were collected in experiments that did not contextualize the images presented to participants, who were unaware both of the identity of the faces shown to them and of the reason behind their expressions (Hess and Fischer 2013, 2014). The tendency to imitate the expressions and movements of others is heavily influenced by social factors (e.g. whether or not the subjects belong to the same social group: Bourgeois and Hess 2008, Van der Schalk et al. 2011; cooperation or competition: Weyers et al. 2009) as well as by cultural factors (e.g. whether the subject with whom one interacts is good or bad: Likowski et al. 2008), which can even interfere with neural activity (as shown by the increased activation of the anterior cingulate cortex both when we experience pain ourselves and when we see another suffer, provided he or she belongs to our own ethnic group: Xu et al. 2009). All this shows that imitation plays an important role in regulating intersubjective behaviour, and should not be viewed as the automatic outcome of a perceptual process, but rather as a reaction that depends on the way in which the stimulus is interpreted within the context in which it occurs.

Part II

Part II

Experience

James

From the standpoint of subjective experience, it is undoubtedly the case that when we are in the grip of an emotion we *feel* something. Common sense usually considers these feelings as consequences of a given emotional state: we get scared and we tremble; we get embarrassed and we feel a rush of blood to the face and so on. In short, on a common-sense view an emotion consists in the perception of a given event and causes certain physical symptoms. The scheme would be as follows:

stimulus → interpretation → emotion → bodily reaction.

In his 'What is an Emotion?', published in 1884, American psychologist and pragmatist philosopher William James suggested quite a different reading. James's approach is revolutionary because it changes the order of the elements in the sequence; the ideation or perception of the stimulus, on his reading, is directly followed by physiological alterations. According to James, emotions amount to our experiencing and *feeling* these alterations. The revised scheme would thus appear as follows:

stimulus → interpretation → bodily reaction → emotion.

James's contribution to the debate on emotions is not limited to 'What is an emotion?'. In fact, the theme of emotions is a recurring one throughout his philosophical work – in particular in chapter XXV of

Principles of Psychology (which also includes the 1884 text) and 'The Physical Basis of Emotion', a paper published in 1894. Nonetheless, it is in 'What is an Emotion?' that we find what is normally considered the most representative statement of James's theory of emotions:

> Our natural way of thinking about these standard emotions is that the mental perception of some fact excites the mental affection called the emotion, and that this latter state of mind gives rise to the bodily expression. My thesis on the contrary is that *the bodily changes follow directly the* PERCEPTION *of the exciting fact, and that our feeling of the same changes as they occur* IS *the emotion.* Common sense says, we lose our fortune, are sorry and weep; we meet a bear, are frightened and run; we are insulted by a rival, are angry and strike. The hypothesis here to be defended says that this order or sequence is incorrect, that the one mental state is not immediately induced by the other, that the bodily manifestations must first be interposed between, and that the more rational statement is that we feel sorry because we cry, angry because we strike, afraid because we tremble, and not that we cry, strike, or tremble, because we are sorry, angry, or fearful, as the case may be. Without the bodily states following on the perception, the latter would be purely cognitive in form, pale, colourless, destitute of emotional warmth. We might then see the bear, and judge it best to run, receive the insult and deem it right to strike, but we could not actually *feel* afraid or angry. (James 1884: 189–90)

James uses the qualification 'standard' to refer to emotions characterized by a visible or, at least, subjectively perceptible physical symptomatology. He observes that some ideations and perceptions are accompanied by pleasant or unpleasant sensations which are, however, not intense enough to cause experienceable and measurable physiological alterations (e.g. acceleration of heartbeat or respiratory rate), nor to trigger body movements or changes in facial expressions. In this paper, James focuses exclusively on 'standard emotions'. Still, by sketching the distinction between 'coarse' and 'subtle' emotions, on which he will expand in greater detail in *the Principles of Psychology*,[1] James does devote some thought to what he calls 'the moral, intellectual and aesthetic feelings', that is to those instances of pleasure and pain that seem to be 'genuinely cerebral'. To be sure, when we appreciate the beauty of a mathematical demonstration or admire an act of justice, we seem to experience emotions without physical symptoms. And yet,

> Unless in them there actually be coupled with the intellectual feeling a bodily reverberation of some kind, unless we actually laugh at the neatness of the mechanical device, thrill at the justice of the act, or tingle at the perfection of the musical form, our mental condition is more allied to a judgment of *right* than to anything else. And such a judgment is rather to be classed among awareness of truth: it is a *cognitive* act. But as a matter of fact the intellectual feeling hardly ever does exist thus unaccompanied. (James 1884: 201–2)

The body is therefore necessarily involved in affective phenomena. James shows an inclusive attitude towards physical alterations that constitute emotions. Autonomic, metabolic and hormonal reactions as well as muscular activity (i.e. the so-called expressive movements, instrumental behaviour, inclinations to act, etc.) contribute to the bodily feedback that generates emotional feelings:

> More and more, as physiology advances, we begin to discern how almost infinitely numerous and subtle they [the bodily affections characteristic of any one of the standard emotions] must be. . . . not only the heart, but the entire circulatory system, forms a sort of sounding-board, which every change of our consciousness,

however slight, may make reverberate. Hardly a sensation comes to us without sending waves of alternate constriction and dilatation down the arteries of our arms. The blood-vessels of the abdomen act reciprocally with those of the more outward parts. The bladder and bowels, the glands of the mouth, throat, and skin, and the liver, are known to be affected gravely in certain severe emotions, and are unquestionably affected transiently when the emotions are of a lighter sort. That the heart-beats and the rhythm of breathing play a leading part in all emotions whatsoever, is a matter too notorious for proof. And what is really equally prominent, but less likely to be admitted until special attention is drawn to the fact, is the continuous co-operation of the voluntary muscles in our emotional states. Even when no change of outward attitude is produced, their inward tension alters to suit each varying mood, and is felt as a difference of tone or of strain. In depression the flexors tend to prevail; in elation or belligerent excitement the extensors take the lead. And the various permutations and combinations of which these organic activities are susceptible, make it abstractly possible that no shade of emotion, however slight, should be without a bodily reverberation as unique, when taken in its totality, as is the mental mood itself. (James 1884: 191–2)

Can one fancy the state of rage and picture no ebullition of it in the chest, no flushing of the face, no dilatation of the nostrils, no clenching of the teeth, no impulse to vigorous action . . .? (James 1884: 194)

Objects of rage, love, fear, etc., not only prompt a man to outward deeds, but provoke characteristic alterations in his attitude and visage, and affect his breathing, circulation, and other organic functions in specific ways. When the outward deeds are inhibited, these latter emotional expressions still remain, and we read the anger in the face, though the blow may not be struck, and the fear betrays itself in voice and color, though one may suppress all other sign. (James 1890.ii: 442)

[Carl Lange and William James] affirmed it [emotional consciousness] to be the effect of the organic changes, muscular and visceral, of which the so called 'expression' of the emotion consists. (James [1894] 1994: 205)[2]

On some occasions, however, James seems to be placing exclusive emphasis on autonomic feedback when it comes to defining what counts as the constitutive dimension of emotion (e.g. James 1890.ii: 465: 'The *visceral and organic* part . . . on this it is probable that the chief part of the felt emotion depends' and James [1894] 1994: 207: 'Visceral factors . . . seem to be the most essential ones of all'). By doing this, he seems to minimize the role played by expressive and instrumental behaviour within emotional experience.[3] The paramount importance (allegedly) attached by James to autonomic nervous system activity is the critical target of many of his theoretical opponents, including American physiologist Walter Cannon, who in a 1927 article entitled 'The James-Lange Theory of Emotions: A Critical Examination and an Alternative Theory' raised five objections against James's view. First, dissection of the spinal cord and vagus nerve does not significantly affect emotional behaviour, as Cannon himself demonstrated in experiments on cats (Cannon, Lewis and Britton 1927). Moreover, the general visceral afferent fibres are relatively insensitive, the reaction times of the smooth muscles are rather long, and the artificial induction of certain autonomic changes (e.g. by injections of adrenaline) does not lead to the affective states to which these normally correspond.[4] The most significant objection, however, concerns the fact that many of the autonomic changes that are symptomatic of a given emotion can also occur in its absence: for example, one can shiver as much from cold as from fear; both a hypoglycaemic crisis and terror cause excessive sweating, pallor and tachycardia; nausea is typical of both disgust and indigestion. This line of criticism had already been put forward by William L. Worcester (1893) and David Irons (1894), to whom James replied in 'The Physical Basis of Emotion', arguing that the physical symptoms that can be linked to an emotion include a broader set of autonomic alterations than those considered by his critics ('Visceral factors, hard to localize, are left out', James [1894] 1994: 207). And yet not only does he fail to specify which 'visceral factors' Worcester and Irons purportedly failed to examine; he also adds that these factors 'seem to be the most essential ones of all' (James [1894] 1994: 207). Such a qualification further supports the view that his theory is committed to assigning a key role to the autonomic nervous system in the formation of emotions.

James makes a less controversial claim when he argues that bodily changes attributable to emotions do not produce an undifferentiated state of arousal, but are 'almost infinitely numerous and subtle' (James 1884: 191). In many cases they are visible alterations, which constitute expressions and behaviour, while in other cases they may be invisible and yet felt by the subject. It is this 'being felt' of alterations that constitutes emotion: 'Every one of the bodily changes, whatsoever it be, is *felt*, acutely or obscurely, the moment it occurs' (James 1884: 192). James puts forward three core arguments in support of this thesis. The first and most famous consists in the speculative experiment 'of subtracting certain elements of feeling from an emotional state supposed to exist in its fulness, and saying what the residual elements are' (James 1884: 193):

If we fancy some strong emotion, and then try to abstract from our consciousness of it all the feelings of its characteristic bodily symptoms, we find that we have nothing left behind, no 'mind-stuff' out of which the emotion can be constituted, and that a cold and neutral state of intellectual perception is all that remains. (James 1884: 193)

If we deprive an emotional episode of its characteristic feelings, we ultimately end up losing sight of the emotion altogether: 'A purely disembodied human emotion is a nonentity. . . . emotion dissociated from all bodily feeling is inconceivable' (James 1884: 194).

In the light of the 'subtraction argument', James's claim that '*the bodily changes follow directly the* PERCEPTION *of the exciting fact, and . . . our feeling of the same changes as they occur* IS *the emotion*' (James 1884: 189–90) implies that the somatic effects that the object of the emotion arouses in the subject are a necessary condition of the emotion itself. But does James also think of them as a sufficient one? According to his second argument, the answer seems to be yes:

Panic is increased by flight, and . . . the giving way to the symptoms of grief or anger increases those passions themselves. . . . Refuse to express a passion, and it dies. . . . Whistling to keep up courage is no mere figure of speech. On the other hand, sit all day in a moping posture, sigh, and reply to everything with a dismal voice, and your melancholy lingers. . . . if we wish to conquer undesirable emotional tendencies in ourselves, we must assiduously, and in the first instance cold-bloodedly, go through the *outward motions* of those contrary dispositions we prefer to cultivate. (James 1884: 197–8)

The phenomenon of bodily feedback to which James here refers entails the idea that physiological alterations are the *cause* (and, in this sense, a necessary and sufficient condition) of emotions. The same thesis, which is restated with quite some emphasis elsewhere (e.g. 'The more closely I scrutinise my states, the more persuaded I become, that whatever moods, affections, and passions I have, are in very truth constituted by, and made up of, those bodily changes we ordinarily call their expression or consequence; . . . the emotion is nothing but the feeling of the reflex bodily effects of what we call its "object"' in James 1884: 194, and 'the general causes of the emotions are indubitably physiological' in James 1890 ii: 449), underlies James's third argument, namely the observation that the origin of the emotions of patients suffering from mental disorders is often exclusively bodily in nature, so that emotions come about and persist even though they lack any object whatsoever.

Having ascertained the crucial role of the perception of bodily changes in the generation of an emotional episode, we still need to determine where these 'almost infinitely numerous and subtle' bodily changes come from. With respect to this issue, James's analysis in 'What is an Emotion?' is rather elusive and confines itself to describing the transition from perception to emotion:

> An object falls on a sense-organ and is apperceived by the appropriate cortical centre; or else the latter, excited in some other way, gives rise to an idea of the same object. Quick as a flash, the reflex currents pass down through their pre-ordained channels, alter the condition of muscle, skin and viscus; and these alterations, apperceived like the original object, in as many specific portions of the cortex, combine with it in consciousness and transform it from an object-simply-apprehended into an object-emotionally-felt. (James 1884: 203)

As several critics soon pointed out, James does not specify what exactly 'perception of the exciting fact' amounts to, nor does he explain the reason why ideations and perceptions should cause specific bodily changes. It is also not clear, among other things, how it is possible that the same stimulus sometimes produces opposite symptoms in different individuals (or even in the same individual at different times).

In 'The Physical Basis of Emotion', James tackles each of these objections, starting with the criticism put forward by Wilhelm Wundt (1891), William Worcester (1893) and David Irons (1894), who point out that emotional reactions are not determined by the object per se, but rather by the way in which the subject relates to it. A wild beast can be a source of terror if encountered in the woods, and of curiosity if observed in the zoo: emotion implies some form of evaluation of the exciting facts, and this is something that James seems to entirely neglect. James replies as follows:

> A reply to these objections is the easiest thing in the world to make
> . . . . 'Objects' are certainly the primitive arousers of instinctive reflex movements. But they take their place, as experience goes on, as elements in total 'situations'. (James [1894] 1994: 206)

Later on James also specifies that in his view the 'objective content' of perception includes 'judgments as well as elements judged' (James [1894] 1994: 208). Essentially, the idea is that the 'perception of the exciting fact' does not merely amount to the sensory registration of an external stimulus: each stimulus is rather contextualized in holistic 'situations' and it is these, and not the stimuli as such, that constitute the 'exciting facts'. This means that emotions are underpinned by bodily changes which, being responses to the perception of stimuli, embody a specific evaluative attitude. While his critics surreptitiously assume that perception and evaluation are two distinct phases of the interaction between organism and environment, James seems to reject the idea of a separation between feelings and cognitive processes: physiological alterations, which we perceive as having affective connotations, already presuppose the prior, pre-reflexive attribution of value and meaning. It is not accidental that James develops his philosophical analysis within the framework of a Darwinian approach to biology and physiology (James 1884: 190–1): emotions are reactive processes triggered by way of interaction with certain environmental factors, and the perception of bodily changes represents the tool that guides the organism through a world imbued with meaning.

However, James notes that the intrinsically evaluative character of the physiological alterations that constitute emotions does not entail any unequivocal correspondence between each and every emotion and the physiological alterations that constitute it, nor between an emotion and its specific instances. The assessment of the presence of a danger, for example, can unfold at the bodily level in different ways depending on the type of danger, or, more generally, on the surrounding context broadly construed (i.e. if it is raining and we are afraid of getting wet, we will start to run for cover; if we come across a wild beast during a walk in the woods, we will be paralysed with fear; etc.). However, although they can vary significantly, the symptoms of a given emotion are always expressed on a continuous spectrum of functional similarity, and it is on this basis that it is possible to interpret different phenomena in the light of the same emotional category, without thereby downplaying their multifaceted complexity: 'If one should seek to name each particular one of them of which the human heart is the seat, it is plain that the limit to their number would lie in the introspective vocabulary of the seeker, each race of men having found names for some shade of feeling which other races have left undiscriminated' (James 1890 ii: 485).

James's appreciation of the plurality and variety of the manifestations of emotions is accompanied, on the one hand, by his tendency to regard affective states not as discrete entities, but rather as flows of experience ('Surely there is no definite affection of "anger" in an "entitative" sense': James [1894] 1994: 206), and, on the other, by a certain degree of hostility to classifications and taxonomies.[5]

'So long as they [the emotions] are set down as so many eternal and sacred psychic entities . . ., so long all that *can* be done with them is reverently to catalogue their separate characters, points, and effects', he writes. 'Is there no way out from this level of individual description in the case of the emotions? I believe there is a way out, but I fear that few will take it' (James 1890 ii: 449).

Somatic theory of emotions

In recent years, new experimental methods have made it possible to substantiate James's intuition about the centrality of bodily dimension to emotional experience. In a neuroimaging study published in 2000, for example, Damasio and colleagues highlighted a strong link between self-induced experiences of happiness, sorrow, anger and fear, and specific patterns of activation of brain areas (insula, secondary somatosensory cortex, anterior and posterior cingulate cortex, hypothalamus and nuclei in the brainstem tegmentum) involved in the mapping and regulation of bodily states (Damasio et al. 2000).[6] It was in fact Damasio who first resumed and built upon James's theory of emotions, from which, however, the Portuguese neuroscientist distanced himself on quite a number of issues – including, as we shall see, the irreducibility of emotions to the feelings of emotions, the possibility of endogenous activation of the brain's somatosensory system and the need to adequately consider the role played by evaluative processes in the generation of emotions.

Damasio represents the homeostatic system in the form of a tree whose trunk is made up of metabolic processes, immune responses and basic reflexes common to every living organism; moving higher up, towards the branches, we find the behavioural responses to reward and punishment, followed by drives and motivations. At the top,

Damasio places the so-called 'emotions proper' (i.e. 'emotions in the narrow sense of the term – from joy and sorrow and fear, to pride and shame and sympathy', Damasio 2003: 34) and feelings, which are the exclusive prerogative of the (evolutionarily) most sophisticated organisms (equipped with a nervous system, etc.). However, even a paramecium swimming towards the sector of its bath with the highest concentration of nutrients demonstrates the ability to react emotionally. After all, in Damasio's view an emotion is first and foremost a mechanism for identifying events and stimuli to be either avoided as threats or exploited as opportunities. Being a mechanism geared to the survival and well-being of the organism, emotion exists in all forms of life. Based on the assumption that emotion consists in establishing a sensible link between the eliciting stimulus and cognitive and behavioural reactions, Damasio defines their 'essence' as follows:

> the collection of changes in body states that are induced in myriad organs by nerve cell terminals, under the control of a dedicated brain system, which is responding to the content of thoughts relative to a particular entity or event. (Damasio 1994: 139)

The perception of the bodily changes that constitute emotion is what Damasio calls the feeling of emotion. Unlike James, he maintains that emotion is not reducible to the feeling of emotion. This is an important novelty, which allows Damasio to extend emotional capacity beyond the limits of consciousness, both at the level of the individual (as nervous responses to physical changes may occur without the subject feeling anything) and at the level of the different species (as emotion emerges even from the behaviour of simple organisms, such as a paramecium or a bacterium). On the other hand, the conscious perception of the bodily changes that constitute emotion makes it possible to plan one's interactions with the environment as well as to generalize information concerning – say – the risks and benefits of some given stimuli and situations, and makes, in general, room for a certain degree of flexibility of response (Damasio 1994: 133). The 'essence' of feeling, in general, is 'an idea – an idea of the body, its interior, in certain circumstances' (Damasio 2003: 88) and feelings of emotion consist in perceiving certain physical states and in establishing a correlation between the perception of these states and specific thoughts, perceptions or ideations. In the case of primary emotions (happiness, sadness, anger, fear and disgust), the relevant feelings correspond to pre-organized modules of bodily response; in the case of their variants (e.g. ecstasy and euphoria for happiness, melancholy and wistfulness for sorrow, panic and shyness for fear), they depend instead on the association of a cognitive content with the modification of a pre-organized module of bodily response.

Damasio also discusses the possibility that the feeling of emotion may emerge from the representation of physical alterations that do not actually take place, as if they took place. In any such case, the neural centres associated with the corresponding bodily changes would be activated even in the absence of such changes. This 'as-if loop', which is supposed to spare the body the energy otherwise required to accommodate real changes, would have evolved through the acquisition, by means of direct experience, of a relatively large set of associations between certain images and perceptions and corresponding bodily states. In a note to his 1884 essay, William James envisaged a similar situation when he referred to 'cases of morbid fear in which objectively the heart is not much perturbed. . . . it is of course possible that the cortical centres normally percipient of dread as a complex of cardiac and other organic sensations due to real bodily change, should become *primarily* excited in bran-disease, and give rise to an hallucination of the changes being there, – an hallucination of dread, consequently, coexistent with a comparatively calm pulse, &c. I say it is possible, for I am ignorant of observations which might test the fact' (James 1884: 199–200). In any event, Damasio introduces the idea that the brain can be activated in the same way as it is activated when certain physical changes occur, but without these occurring – a view that is clearly at odds with the centrality of 'the body as theater' of James's theory (Damasio 1994: 155). To date, the idea of an 'as if' loop is still a hypothesis. Damasio himself acknowledges that the brain is probably unable to predict in detail the conditions of the body following the release of a large number of neural and chemical signals, and admits that the subjective phenomenology of an 'as if' experience is bound to be different from that of the feeling of actual physical changes (Damasio 1994: 159).

A further criticism levelled by Damasio holds that James failed to give due weight to the evaluative processes involved in emotional experience (Damasio 1994: 129–31). Thus, while James's theory does explain what Damasio calls 'primary emotions', that is innate and pre-organized response modules that depend in particular on the amygdala, it cannot account for 'secondary emotions', which result instead from a deliberate and conscious consideration of the relevant stimuli (followed by automatic responses elaborated by the prefrontal cortex on the basis of memory, previous experience and associations; these responses are signalled to the amygdala and to the anterior cingulate cortex, which are the centres involved in the generation of primary emotions, and which in turn respond by effecting chemical and sensorimotor alterations; Damasio 1994: 136–8). As we already mentioned, the failure to properly flesh out the link between emotions and evaluations has often been regarded as the main weakness of William James's theory. Damasio, instead, takes this link seriously and is especially interested in understanding how the ability to make good decisions depends on a correct affective perception of the values at stake in a given situation, which led him to formulate the so-called 'somatic marker hypothesis' (see below, Debate II, in particular pp. 103–9).

Alternatives and criticism
Emotions and values

Emotions and formal objects

In the 1960s and 1970s, the focus of psychological and philosophical debates gradually shifted from the bodily dimension of emotional experience to the 'cognitive' evaluation of its eliciting conditions. Taking its distance from the dominant approaches of the first half of the century – and in particular as a reaction to the Jamesian identification of emotions with the feeling of bodily changes, as well as to the behaviouristic reduction of emotions to bodily 'pattern reactions' (e.g. Watson 1919) – the new 'cognitivist' perspective focused on the relationship between individuals, their emotions, and the intentional properties of those emotions (i.e. what they are about). This strategy aims to address some of the issues that previous theories had left unanswered. For example, the behaviourist model of the stimulus–response mechanism is unable to account for the possibility that the same stimulus can cause different emotions in different individuals, or even in the same individual at different times. Furthermore, William James's theory does not sufficiently engage with the question of what initiates the emotional process. At the same time, the equivalence between emotions and feelings of bodily changes is problematic for a number of reasons: on the one hand, there are feelings that are not emotions, such as hunger or itch; on the other hand, some physiological alterations that are typical of an emotion (e.g. the acceleration of the heartbeat when one is in love or nausea when one feels disgust) can also occur in non-affectively relevant situations (e.g. when running up the stairs or suffering from indigestion). According to psychologist Magda Arnold, the main difference between feelings and emotions lies in the fact that the former signal only the hedonic quality of our reaction to a given stimulus, whereas the latter constitute a much more complex phenomenon and reveal the overall attitude that characterizes our interaction with a given stimulus (Arnold 1960: 20–1). On this basis, Arnold stresses that the analysis of the subjective phenomenology of emotion ought to be coupled with that of the relationship between subject and environment, so as to investigate the link between emotions and their objects:

> In emotion . . . there is not only someone who experiences but also someone or something that occasions the experience. We are afraid of something, we rejoice over something, we love someone, we are angry at something or someone. Emotion seems to have an object . . . . To say that emotion may be vague and objectless, as in neurotic anxiety or in depression, is to confuse the issue. There are departures from normal functioning. Normal emotion carries with it the reference to an object or situation that is known in some way. (Arnold 1960: 170)

In the contemporary debate there is a broad consensus about the intentional dimension of emotions. That is to say, scholars generally agree that, at least in most cases, emotions are 'about' something: we are afraid *of a wild beast*, we are proud *of our success*, we fear *that the worst will happen*, we love *our parents* and so on. These are referred to as the 'particular objects' of emotions, that is what a given emotion is directed to in each of its specific instances.[1] I can be afraid of a snake, of war, of falling down the stairs, and I can admire bravery, sunsets and works of art. Still, these *particular objects* do not exhaust all possible cases of fear and admiration. Moreover, it seems that emotions are not simply directed towards these (or other) objects, but also imply a specific way of interpreting them: if a snake scares me, this means I consider it (viz. I perceive it, judge it, represent it) as potentially dangerous. Similarly, if I feel ashamed because I was just caught naked in public or cheating, that is because I consider these circumstances to be detrimental to my image and reputation. Between those who experience the emotion and the object to which their emotion is directed there is therefore a meaningful relation. It is natural then to ask whether there is a category of 'objects' that is shared by all the experiential instances of a given emotion and that defines the meaning of the relationship between the subject and the object of that emotion: for example, is there something that all experiences of fear have in common *qua* experiences of fear? Those who answer this question in the affirmative usually appeal to the concept of *formal object* and identify VALUE as the *formal object* of emotions. Let φ be a verb that expresses an act: unlike the *particular object* of φing (which is any entity that φ can refer to: for instance, a wild beast, war and falling down the stairs are all particular objects of my being afraid), the *formal object* of φ is 'the object under that description which must apply to it if it is to be possible to φ it. If only what is P can be φd, then "thing which is P" gives the formal object of φing' (Kenny 1963: 132). A *formal object* must be abstract enough to be exemplifiable by a multitude of *particular objects*, and VALUES seem to provide a characterization both of EMOTIONS as a general class and of the subcategories that pertain to it (FEAR, JOY, SHAME, ANGER, etc.). It is important to keep in mind that, in this context, the term 'value' is understood in a neutral sense and includes both positive axiological properties (such as generosity, beauty and kindness) and negative ones (such as selfishness, ugliness and insolence).

Identifying values as *formal objects of* emotions has some advantages. First, assigning a formal object to the act of φing means introducing clear-cut criteria that narrow down the set of eligible instances of φ: for example, only what is past can be remembered, only what is not owned can be stolen, only what is dirty can be cleaned, and so on. The same is true of emotions: if VALUE as a *formal object* identifies EMOTION in general, then each of its articulations will match a specific kind of emotion – so that DANGER will be associated with fear, LOSS with sorrow, OFFENCE with anger and so on: 'The specific formal object associated with a given emotion is essential to the definition of that particular emotion' (de Sousa 1987: 122; see also Lyons 1980: 62–3 and 100–1). It is important to bear in mind that the thesis according to which the *formal object* is what allows us to distinguish different kinds of emotion (e.g. de Sousa 1987: 126, 'each emotion type is a unique species defined by its formal object') can also be formulated in a weaker version. One can simply claim that the identification of the *formal object* is not in itself sufficient to distinguish different kinds of emotion, since for instance both shame and contempt seem to share the value of WORTHLESSNESS as their formal object. It may therefore become necessary to consider other aspects as well (such as phenomenological, doxastic, behavioural factors, etc.; see Teroni 2007: 401–3). Second, it is on the basis of its relation to a certain value that an emotional experience becomes intelligible:

> If a man says that he feels remorse for the actions of someone quite unconnected with him, or is envious of his own vices, we are at a loss to understand him. It is, of course, quite possible for someone

to be grateful for a physical injury, if he regards it as having done him some good . . . It is also possible to be proud of a vice or a crime or a defect, if one can represent it to oneself as a virtue or an achievement or an advantage . . . What is not possible is to be grateful for, or proud of, something which one regards as an evil unmixed with good. Again, it is possible to be envious of one's own fruit trees; but only if one mistakenly believes that the land on which they stand is part of one's neighbour's property . . . What is not possible is to envy something which one believes to belong to oneself, or to feel remorse for something in which one believes one had no part. (Kenny 1963: 134–5)

The intelligibility of an emotion thus lies in its intentional relation to a specific axiological property: for example, anger is intelligible in relation to OFFENCE (but not to DANGER, nor to BEAUTY), while pride is intelligible in relation to SUCCESS (but not to LOSS, nor to OFFENCE), and so on. Finally, the link between emotions and values as *formal objects* makes it possible to assess their appropriateness, that is, to raise the question as to whether the *particular object* of a given emotional episode really instantiates the specific value of that emotion. In non-philosophical terms, the question of appropriateness emerges in our everyday life whenever we discuss the reasons behind our emotions and those of others: 'I am angry: what you did offended me', 'Don't be afraid of my dog: it's not dangerous' and so on.

Appraisal theories

At the beginning of the 1960s, Magda Arnold introduced the notion of appraisal precisely in response to the need to investigate the link between emotions and values, to which James's philosophical account paid little attention, and which was essentially ignored by behavioural theories in psychology. For Arnold, appraisal is what lies at the origin of emotional experience: 'To arouse an emotion, the object must be appraised as affecting me in some way, affecting me personally as an individual with my particular experience and my particular aims' (Arnold 1960: 171). However, this appraisal process does not emerge from abstract thought, but is rather the outcome of a pre-reflexive, immediate sense judgement that can be conceptualized by analogy with the notion of direct apprehension in the psychology of perception:

> Psychologists of an earlier generation distinguished between direct apprehension like the *simple seeing* of a color (e.g., blue), *recognizing* it when seeing it on different occasions, and *reflectively knowing* it to be blue. They called both direct and reflective recognition (both of which imply judgements) *apperception*, and distinguished this from *direct apprehension*. But they did not distinguish direct recognition which does not involve rational judgment from reflective recognition which does. Similarly, no great attention was paid to the difference between judgments that *connect* concrete particular sense data with concrete particular objects or events in a given sense experience, and judgments that *generalize* from these sense data or events. Thus it has come about that 'sense' judgments, which merely *find* the relation between sense data, and reflective judgments, that *understand* them, are both called judgments, and often included in the term 'perception'. Yet there is a significant difference between the two . . . What we call *appraisal* or *estimate* is close to . . . a sense judgment. (Arnold 1960: 174–5)

Sometimes the appraisal is supplemented by a reflective judgement ('secondary evaluation'), in which case the emotional experience will undergo some changes in accordance with the newly emerging evaluation. Although in Arnold's view an appraisal is something direct and intuitive, it is not a dimension of perceptual experience, but rather a distinct process that complements sense perception and provides the motivation required to act by generating attraction or repulsion: 'appraisal makes possible an active approach, acceptance or withdrawal, and thus establishes our relationship to the outside world' (Arnold 1960: 176). It seems that appraisal performs the essential function of generating the emotional process, while the more body-specific aspects emerge later:

> Emotion must be aroused by the individual's perception and appreciation of some situation, while physiological changes though important, play a secondary role. Since such physiological changes are not reflexes, they themselves must be initiated by perception and appraisal. (Arnold 1960: 143)

In this sense, Arnold attributes to the appraisal process the primary role of eliciting both bodily and behavioural changes and the experience of emotion itself.

Arnold nonetheless maintains that the phenomenon of emotion cannot come down to the appraisal component alone. A suitable theory must be able to integrate the psychological, neurological, and physiological aspects of affective phenomena (Arnold 1960: v), taking into account the activation patterns of the autonomic nervous system that are specific to each emotion, as well as feelings and behaviour: 'We can now define emotion as *the felt tendency toward anything intuitively appraised as good (beneficial), or away from anything intuitively appraised as bad (harmful). This attraction or aversion is accompanied by a pattern of physiological changes organized toward approach or withdrawal. The patterns differ for different emotions*' (Arnold 1960: 182).

The notion of appraisal was further developed by Richard Lazarus, from his 1966 study entitled *Psychological Stress and the Coping*

Process to the complete formulation of the cognitive–motivational–relational theory of emotions laid out in his *Emotion and Adaptation* (1991). Like Arnold, Lazarus views appraisal as the evaluation of the meaning of our interactions with the environment in relation to our interests and expectations (e.g. Lazarus 1991: 121, 144 and 2001: 40). This evaluation, which Lazarus terms 'cognitive' in a broad sense, so as to include abstract, reflective and deliberate thought processes as well as pre-reflective and automatic modes of meaning generation, unfolds on two levels. The 'primary appraisal' process is concerned with the importance of the interaction from the point of view of our subjective well-being (i.e. is this a threat or an opportunity?) and proceeds along the lines of 'goal relevance' (i.e. is there something at stake that promotes or hinders my goals?), 'goal congruence or incongruence' (i.e. is this an obstacle or a benefit?) and 'type of personal involvement' (i.e. the nature of my interests in the specific circumstances, e.g. my moral values, my ideals, my social role and my well-being or that of others: see Lazarus 2001: 58). 'Secondary appraisal' concerns instead coping and adaptation strategies and involves assessing who or what is responsible for a given harm or good ('blame and credit for an outcome'), whether or not we can take advantage of the opportunity or else escape from the harm or minimize it ('coping potential') and what the implications are for the future ('future expectations'). Both the primary and the secondary appraisal levels are constantly enriched with new information by virtue of feedback mechanisms. The appraisal process is therefore recursive and constantly feeds in estimates and new considerations, cast in the form of 'reappraisals'. It is both the cause of emotion and its constitutive element (Lazarus 1991: Chapter 5).

At the level of each appraisal component, a 'partial meaning' emerges (Lazarus 2001: 64) that can only be understood insofar as 'the two complex subsystems, person and environment, are conjoined and considered at a new level of analysis. The separate identities of the two subsystems are then lost in favour of an emergent condition, described as one or another relationship with its own relational meaning' (Lazarus 1991: 90). The integration of these 'partial meanings' into a higher-level synthetic unit is what Lazarus calls the 'core relational theme':

> A core relational theme is simply the central (hence core) relational harm or benefit in adaptational encounters that underlies each specific kind of emotion. There are diverse kinds of harmful relationships, each of which constitutes a core relational theme leading to a distinctive negative emotion. There are also different kinds of beneficial relationships, each of which constitutes a core relational theme leading to a distinctive positive emotion. (Lazarus 1991: 121)

Lazarus considers emotions as discrete categories and defines each of them in terms of its distinctive core relational theme: for example, 'a demeaning offense against me and mine' in relation to anger, 'having transgressed a moral imperative' in relation to guilt, 'having experienced an irrevocable loss' in relation to sorrow, 'wanting what someone else has' in relation to envy, 'being moved by another's suffering and wanting to help' in relation to compassion and so on (Lazarus 1991: 122 and 2001: 64).

Lazarus's emphasis on the relational nature of appraisal, which emerges from the interaction between subject and environment, is supplemented by the crucial role played by our interests and goals. The motivational dimension of our experience is also essential for understanding the appraisal process that lies at the origin of the phenomenon of emotions. Finally, on the cognitive level, Lazarus distinguishes between knowledge, which concerns what an individual knows or believes, in either general or specific circumstances, and which can be expressed at different degrees of cognitive complexity (consciously or unconsciously, explicitly or tacitly, etc.), and appraisal, which represents a personal evaluation of the meaning of such knowledge and beliefs in the context of a specific episode of interaction between the individual and the environment (Lazarus 1991: 144–9). Appraisal plays the key adaptive role of turning information into *meaning* – and it is by virtue of this transformation that experience acquires the affective tone that is typical of emotions (Lazarus 2001: 58).

A further theory built around appraisal mechanisms is Klaus Scherer's component process model (Scherer 1984, 2001, 2009), which characterizes emotions as patterns of synchronization of five components: cognition, which is in charge of appraisal processes; the autonomic activity necessary for regulating the organism; motivation, which prepares for action; motor and expressive activity, which makes communication possible; and subjective feelings, required for monitoring the interaction between organism and environment. The appraisal component is in turn divided into distinct processes in charge of evaluating different aspects of the interaction (relevance, implications, coping potential, normative meaning), which Scherer calls 'Stimulus Evaluation Checks' (SECs) and which collect information about our ability to control or manage a given event, assess whether it is pleasant or painful, relevant or irrelevant to our interests and so on. Like Lazarus, Scherer describes the appraisal process as recursive and dynamic, but introduces the further hypothesis that SECs occur in a linear sequence: different sequences result in different emotions, characterized by specific, interdependent and interconnected configurations of the five components of which they consist.

The models of Arnold, Lazarus and Scherer, as well as other theoretical approaches in the contemporary appraisal tradition, interpret emotions as processes consisting of a set of mutually interacting components. From a psychological and cognitive standpoint, there are two main views about appraisal mechanisms. Some believe that these depend on two different cognitive modes: the first is computational and rule-based, while the other is associative (e.g. Clore and Ortony 2000). In the first case, appraisal would take place in an abstract, propositional and conscious form, while in the second case it would have a perceptual, embodied and spontaneous nature. Other scholars hold that appraisal mechanisms also encompass the activation of sensorimotor responses triggered automatically on the basis of biologically innate response programmes (e.g. Leventhal and Scherer 1987). In general, scholars appear to converge on the view that appraisal is mostly a direct, pre-reflexive and dynamic process. The organism constantly examines itself and the external environment, and constantly reformulates its appraisals on the basis of emerging changes. On the other hand, the dominant componential approach defines appraisal as an element that, within the framework of the emotional process, interacts with other elements (such as physiological activation, behaviour and expression), from which it nonetheless remains distinct. Consequently, the production of meaning implied by appraisal is relatively independent of the overall structure of the psychophysical relation between organism and environment. The appraisal tradition thus upholds a fundamental distinction between the cognitive activity of the organism and its bodily dimension: in this perspective, the cognitive and sensorimotor structures of an organism are not co-constituted, and, despite the emphasis placed on their mutual interactions, it is only to the former that evaluative contents are ultimately traced (see Colombetti 2014: 94–7).

Theories of emotions as value judgements

Another cognitivist strategy for accounting for the relation between emotions and values consists in reducing the former to doxastic phenomena of a specific nature, that is to axiological beliefs or value judgements. Unlike appraisal theories, which regard the evaluative process as either a cause or a component of emotional experience (or both, as in Lazarus's case), theories of emotions as value judgements identify emotion with the evaluative process itself, couched in the terms of a judgement about the axiological properties instantiated by the intentional object:

> [Emotions] are not responses to what happens but evaluations of what happens. And they are not responses to those evaluative judgments but rather they *are* those judgments. (Solomon [1976] 1993: 127; see also Nussbaum 2004)

In the subjectivist version advocated by Robert Solomon in his 1976 monograph entitled *The Passions,* this approach aims to illustrate the perspectival nature of the phenomenon of emotions, namely the fact that they 'are not concerned with *the* world but with *my* world' (Solomon [1976] 1993: 19), and hence that the object they address does not exist per se, but only as an object of affective experience. While he emphasizes the subjective nature of the value judgements in which emotions consist, Solomon also thinks he can explain the desiderative dimension of this kind of experience, insofar as the axiological beliefs in question must directly concern our interests and goals:

> Not all evaluative judgments are emotions. . . . Emotions are self-involved and relatively *intense* evaluative judgments. . . . The judgments and objects that constitute our emotions are those

which are especially important to us, meaningful to us, concerning matters in which we have invested our Selves. (Solomon [1976] 1993: 127)

Conversely, it is not immediately clear how a theory that reduces emotions to sheer doxastic phenomena can explain the relation between emotions and motivation. Solomon's strategy seems to be to attribute a constitutive motivational dimension to the value judgement, which will thus strike the subject involved as particularly 'intense' and meaningful. Not every judgement of value, however, is necessarily motivating. In fact, we may hold an axiological belief concerning something that affects us directly and profoundly and yet not feel in any way compelled to act on it.

A further problem with Solomon's theory emerges from the thesis that, although emotions are typically accompanied by feelings, these feelings are neither necessary nor sufficient to define them or tell them apart. Over the years, however, Solomon has fine-tuned some of the more radically intellectualistic aspects of his theory of emotions. Consider for instance his 'Thoughts and Feelings' (2001):[2] despite insisting that emotions consist in judgements, here Solomon seems inclined to construe the latter broadly, that is as processes that are not necessarily abstract or reflexive in nature. He also admits that the notions of 'cognition' and 'judgement' have to be conceptualized in a way that pays sufficient attention to the experiential aspect of emotions, that is feelings and the role of the body. It is against this background that Solomon introduces the notion of 'judgements of the body':

The judgments that I claim are constitutive of emotion may be nonpropositional and bodily as well as propositional and articulate [. . .]. There are feelings, 'affects' if you like, critical to emotion. But they are not distinct from cognition or judgment, and they

are not mere 'readouts' of processes going on in the body. They are
judgments *of* the body. (Solomon 2003: 159–60)

In general, however, the idea that emotions *are* value judgements is
not persuasive. To begin with, it leaves no room for the possibility that
one may feel an emotion in the absence of an axiological belief. But if
we hold this assumption, then we are committed to denying that – say
– animals and very young children are capable of feeling emotions.
To be sure, in the latest version of his theory Solomon draws upon
a rather broad definition of value judgement, and indeed explicitly
includes the non-reflective and non-deliberate 'judgements' of
animals among the conditions of possibility of emotional experience
(Solomon 2003: 155). Unfortunately, this response accomplishes
little, as the problem resurfaces if we reframe the issue with reference
to those cases in which the subject makes a value judgement and
yet experiences an emotion that does not conform to it. These are
referred to as 'recalcitrant emotions'. A classic example is the fear of
flying, which one continues to experience even though one knows
perfectly well that a plane is safer than – say – the car we drive every
day. In such a scenario, there is no correspondence between the type
of judgement made and the emotion felt. One might try to get around
this problem by assuming that the subject has two contradictory
beliefs: a conscious and deliberate one (i.e. 'the plane is safe'), and
an unconscious and inarticulate one (i.e. 'the plane is dangerous').
This is not a particularly persuasive strategy, but even if one were
to take it at face value, a further question would remain open: for
it is hard to deny that we may formulate a value judgement or belief
about something that is relevant to us without, however, experiencing
the corresponding emotion. In this sense, meeting the cognitive
requirements of the theory may not be a sufficient condition for
an emotion to occur: for how can we distinguish between a value

judgement and a value judgement that constitutes an emotion if the propositional content of the two judgements is the same? Theories of emotions as value judgements prove unable properly to account for the phenomenological dimension of emotional experience, to wit, of emotion as it is *experienced*.

Theories of emotions as perceptions of value

An attempt to reconcile the notion of appraisal with the Jamesian tradition is the so-called 'embodied appraisal' theory. Developed by Jesse Prinz (2004a), this account combines the view that emotions represent the relation between organism and environment from the point of view of the organism's well-being with the thesis that emotions are perceptions of bodily changes. In defence of the idea that emotions are representations, Prinz appeals to Dretske's (1981) teleosemantics, according to which a mental representation is a state that fulfils two conditions: first, it carries information about what it co-occurs with (it is sufficient that the correlation be reliable, and not necessarily invariable; it typically has a causal nature); second, it serves the specific function of carrying such information:

> a mental representation is a mental state that is reliably caused by something and has been set in place by learning or evolution to detect that thing. . . . a mental representation is a mental state that has been set up to be set off by something. (Prinz 2004a: 54)

Emotions co-occur with certain patterns of bodily changes. According to the Jamesian approach, there is indeed a causal correlation between physiological alterations and their perception, that is emotion. However, this is not sufficient to warrant the claim that emotions *represent* bodily changes, as within the framework of Dretske's theory a representation must also display a functional meaning. On the other hand, it makes little sense to assume that the function of emotions is to represent bodily changes per se, as it is not entirely clear what evolutionary advantage we could get from the ability to acquire information about what changes are taking place in our body. When we run away from something, we do not do so because our heartbeat accelerates or because our blood pressure increases. We do so because we are scared. Consequently,

> we should accept the premise that emotions are bodily perceptions but deny that they represent (or exclusively represent) bodily changes. We should insist that emotions detect something more than the vicissitudes of vasculature. Otherwise, they would confer no survival advantage, and we could not make sense of the seemingly intelligible uses to which they are put. (Prinz 2004a: 60)

Prinz claims that emotions represent organism-environment relations, and defines them by resorting to the notion of 'core relational themes' introduced by Lazarus, which, however, he rephrases in a non-conceptual and non-propositional fashion.[3] Emotions are functionally predisposed to be activated by these evaluative properties: in fact, the co-occurrence between the reaction to a core theme and certain patterns of physiological alteration is useful, on an evolutionary level, to prepare the organism to perform an action. Prinz concludes that emotions represent evaluative properties by perceiving bodily changes:

> Emotions track bodily states that reliably cooccur with important organism-environment relations, so emotions reliably cooccur with organism-environment relations. Each emotion is both an internal body monitor and a detector of dangers, threats, losses, or

other matters of concern. Emotions are gut reactions; they use our bodies to tell us how we are faring in the world. (Prinz 2004a: 69)

In conclusion, according to the theory of embodied appraisal, emotions are indirect perceptions of core relational themes: they are perceptions in that they correspond to precise configurations of the somatosensory system of an organism; and they are indirect in that they represent the evaluative properties by virtue of the perception of the bodily changes co-occurring with them (Prinz 2004a: 221–40). In this regard, Prinz introduces an interesting analogy: just as in people with synaesthesia a sensory mode such as sight is activated even upon stimulation of an organ corresponding to another sensory mode (e.g. hearing), so the perception of core themes is concomitant of that of bodily changes. In this sense, the link between emotion and axiological properties is indirect though not inferential; and it is embodied, because it is expressed on the perceptual level:

emotion is a form of perception. Having an emotion is literally perceiving our relationship to the world. . . . we describe emotions as gut reactions. They are like bodily radar detectors that alert us to concerns. When we listen to our emotions, we are not being swayed by meaningless feelings. Nor are we hearing the cold dictates of complex judgments. We are using our bodies to perceive our position in the world. (Prinz 2004a: 240)

While on Prinz's account the equivalence between emotions and perceptions is to be understood in a literal sense, others propose weaker interpretations, according to which this equivalence is merely a comparison (e.g. de Sousa 1987: 149–58) or an analogy, as in the case of Peter Goldie's theory of 'feeling towards' (2000, 2004). Goldie illustrates the importance of feelings in emotional experience by examining their epistemic contribution and by grouping them into two categories: the feeling of one's own bodily state ('bodily feeling') and that directed towards the object of emotion ('feeling towards'). The first type of feelings is a source of knowledge that is both introspective and external: they tell us what the current condition of our body is (e.g. tachycardia or goose pimples), what kind of emotion we are experiencing (e.g. fear), and whether there may be something in the environment that manifests the axiological property that is typical of the emotion we are experiencing (e.g. danger). What bodily feelings do not reveal is the particular object to which our emotion is directed. This is what led Goldie to introduce the notion of 'feeling towards', which involves 'thinking of with feeling', namely a form of involvement, characterized by bodily feelings, with something that goes beyond one's own body (Goldie 2000: 58). It is important to note that 'feeling towards' does not come down to a doxastic attitude (e.g. 'I think this wild beast is dangerous') coupled with the qualitative component of feelings (e.g. 'I am scared by this wild beast'); rather, it is an experience of the world as intrinsically meaningful for the agent:

> The difference between thinking of X as Y without feeling and thinking of X as Y with feeling will not just comprise a different attitude towards the same content – a thinking which earlier was without feeling and now is with feeling. The difference also lies in the content. (Goldie 2000: 60)

To drive this point home, Goldie draws on an analogy with sensory perception to highlight the characteristics of emotional experience, understood as feeling towards, that set it apart from the phenomenon of belief:

> When we respond emotionally to things in the environment, we also, as part of the same experience, typically perceive those things as having the emotion-proper property. (Goldie 2004: 97)

In contrast to beliefs, and similarly to perceptions, emotions have a distinctive phenomenology: one feels something when one experiences them. Moreover, just as in the Müller-Lyer illusion (Figure 1) we can continue to perceive one line as longer than the other even though we know that they are identical, so an emotion can coexist with a belief that justifies the opposite emotion: this is the case for instance of phobias and recalcitrant emotions in general. Emotions can also be ambiguous: we can oscillate between two different modes of feeling towards even in the absence of a proper reason to do so, just as in the ambiguous image of the duck–rabbit (Figure 2) we swing between one form and the other (Goldie 2000: 72–8).

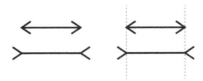

Figure 1 *The Müller-Lyer illusion was presented by German psychiatrist and sociologist Franz Carl Müller-Lyer in 1889 in* Archiv für Anatomie und Physiologie, Physiologische Abteilung.

Figure 2 *The ambiguous figure of the duck–rabbit appeared for the first time anonymously in 'Fliegende Blätter' (1892), with the caption* Welche Thiere gleichen einander am meisten? *(Which animals are most similar?). Source: https://en.wikipedia.org/wiki/Rabbit%E2%80%93duck _illusion#/media/File:Kaninchen_und_Ente.svg.*

A thorough analysis of the analogies between emotions and perceptions is offered by Christine Tappolet (2016), who defines emotions as perceptual experiences of axiological properties. Tappolet believes that emotions, like perceptions, enable us to become aware of certain features of the external world: they are non-conceptual representations of values, which means that they have no propositional content. It follows that emotions do not require possessing the concepts of value that pertain to them: just as it is not necessary to possess the concept of blue to see a blue flower, one can be afraid without possessing the concept of fear. In both perceptual and emotional experience we feel something, and in both cases these are processes that are activated independently of the individual will: I cannot decide to see a blue flower if there isn't any in front of me (though I can picture it in my mind); by the same token, I cannot feel joy just because I want to. Moreover, emotions and perceptions can be recalcitrant, that is, compatible with a scenario in which judgements or beliefs diverge from experience. As we saw, this is the case of phobias and illusions such as Müller-Lyer's. In this sense, emotions and perceptions are said to be 'informationally encapsulated' (Fodor 1983), that is only partially sensitive to the interference of other mental states (knowing that a plane is not a dangerous means of transport has little bearing upon my fear, just as knowing that an oar is straight does not change the fact that, when it is submerged in water, it appears bent).

Tappolet also illustrates what she considers to be the main differences between emotions and perceptions (Tappolet 2016: 24–30). Most of these differences derive from the fact that Tappolet endorses a classical cognitivist and representationalist theory of perception. For example, Tappolet argues that 'unlike sensory experiences, emotions appear closely tied to motivation and action' (Tappolet 2016: 25). The idea that perception and action are two separate and independent processes that follow each other along a linear causal sequence is a typical assumption of classical cognitive science, which today is mostly viewed as problematic (e.g. Varela, Thompson and Rosch 1991; Hurley 1998 and Noë 2004). Indeed, action plays a central role in perceptual experience, for this always implies a sensorimotor understanding of our potential for interaction with the external environment. Several experimental studies suggest that perception and action are neither functionally distinct nor anatomically separate (e.g. Rizzolatti and Matelli 2003), and thus provide evidence in support of concepts such as James Gibson's 'affordance' (1979), and, more generally, action-centred theories of perception, such as enactivist theories (see below, pp. 134–44). Moreover, the quality of our perceptions is heavily influenced by our needs and goals, in the sense that we do not perceive the world-as-it-is, but the world-as-it-is-for-us. Aristotle already noted this when he pointed out that the same smell of food seems delicious when we are hungry and disgusting when we have eaten too much (*De sensu* 443b21–4). In a similar vein, William James observed that the same sensory qualities appear to us differently when we are tired compared to when we are rested, and when we are hungry compared to when we are full (James 1890.ii: 232). More recently, various experiments have shown that, for example, fatigue interferes with the way we perceive the environment. So a slope will appear steeper if we are asked to observe it with a backpack on our shoulders (Proffitt et al. 1995; Proffitt, Creem and Zosh 2001; Bhalla and Proffitt 1999). In the light of these observations, we can take issue with a further difference between emotions and perceptions identified by Tappolet, namely the idea that only the former display hedonic quality, and hence are characterized by either pleasant sensations (as when we are happy or amused) or unpleasant ones (as when we are sad or ashamed) (Tappolet 2016: 25). Still, if perceptual processes do not come down to the registration of external stimuli, but also depend on what matters to the organism (as well as, of course, on the type of sensory apparatus available to the organism and on its performance level), then the axiological meaning of these stimuli will most probably emerge at the sensory level from the initial stages of perception, rather than being the result of some *ex post* evaluation (see, e.g. the 'affective prediction hypothesis' formulated by Barrett and Bar 2009). A further critical issue spotted by Tappolet concerns the fact that while emotions and affective dispositions are susceptible to cultural and social influences, 'our perceptual apparatus appears largely unaffected by cultural and social factors and it hardly changes over the lifetime of individuals' (Tappolet 2016: 27). Again, this is a questionable claim, especially in the light of several experimental studies that show how environmental factors of various nature inform perceptual processes at the subpersonal level by virtue of the phenomenon of brain plasticity (see e.g. Goh and Park 2009 for a discussion on the impact of brain plasticity on perceptual processes, and Gutsell and Inzlicht 2010 for an analysis of the differences in the activation patterns of the motor cortex during the observation of actions performed by members of one's own social group and by members of other social groups). More generally, we know that the category distinctions that are dominant in one's own culture can interfere with perceptual experiences, as confirmed for instance by studies of the interaction between vocabulary and colour perception (for a demonstration of how linguistic categories contribute to speeding up or slowing down perceptual recognition and colour discrimination, see for instance Winawer et al. 2007).

In conclusion, many of the disanalogies between emotion and perception turn out to be only apparent, or in any event less radically problematic than might at first appear, insofar as one rejects the classical representationalist model of perception. It is worth adding that representationalism also poses a problem for the theory of embodied appraisal. We saw that, in support of the thesis on which a given pattern of physiological activation carries information about the meaning of a given stimulus (and thus the perception of the former implies the indirect perception of the latter), Prinz appeals to Dretske's informational semantics and states that the information carried by physiological patterns co-varies with the respective stimuli. This means that if pattern P co-varies with stimulus S, then P is an indicator of S: if the heartbeat tends to accelerate whenever we are in a dangerous situation, then this acceleration is a representation of danger. However, the theory of mental representation on which Prinz's approach is based assumes that the represented content exists independently of the mental state that represents it, which forces Prinz to define core relational themes as objectively existent and ontologically independent of the organism's affective experience (Prinz 2004a: 60–6):

> Fear, for example, may represent the property of being dangerous. Being dangerous, like being poisonous, is a relational property, and a relative property. Something can be dangerous only *to* some creature or other, and whether or not something is dangerous depends on the creature in question. But being dangerous does not depend on being represented as dangerous. Radiation would be dangerous even if we didn't know that it is. Fear represents the property of being dangerous even though that property is possessed by some things that we do not in fact fear. Fear, like sadness, does not represent a response-dependent property. (Prinz 2004a: 63–4)

Fear is probably the emotion that is most germane to the point Prinz wants to make. It is objectively true, for example, that travelling by car is more dangerous than travelling by plane, even though many people are scared at the thought of boarding a plane but not of driving a car (and therefore do not represent travelling by car as dangerous). However, this means that the eliciting conditions of the emotion of fear, as well as the intentional object to which this is directed, do not necessarily coincide with the property of 'danger'. It appears, in fact, that a distinction should be drawn between the *danger* and the *frightening* (i.e. what generates fear).

The fact that emotions are not simply *reactions* to core relational themes understood as objective properties of the environment, and that these themes are rather the outcome of the affectively qualified interpretation and perspective of a given organism is quite evident if we consider cases such as that of pride. It is certainly possible to define the core theme of pride in abstract terms, but the existence of pride as a property of my interactions with the environment will constitutively depend on my expectations, desires, motivations, value system, concerns, needs and so on. The core theme of pride does not exist independently of pride, but rather *emerges together* with pride.

Prinz himself has recently distanced himself from the representationalist approach underlying the theory of embodied appraisal (Schargel and Prinz 2017). We will turn to his revised theory in the third section of this book (see below, pp. 139–42), where we will also discuss other approaches developed within the framework of second-generation cognitive science.

Debate II
Sense and sensibility in decision-making

It is not uncommon to think that emotions are detrimental to good reasoning, and should be expunged from 'rational' decision-making for that reason. Still, an equally common maxim reminds us that the best thing we can do is to 'follow our heart' (understood as the metaphorical seat of emotions). The many studies devoted to the interaction between deliberation and affect in the psychology and neuroscience of decision-making processes show that both the 'rationalist' and the 'romantic' view, while rooted in common-sense, are not cognitively realistic: for emotions inevitably inform, steer and influence our deliberative processes, decisions and choices – and whether or not this is a good thing will depend on the specific circumstances. Antonio Damasio's research has taught us that when reasoning is not supported by affective perceptions due to lesions in the ventromedial region of the brain, our decision-making activity is severely impaired (Damasio, Tranel and Damasio 1991; Damasio 1994, 1996). However, as we will see, Damasio and colleagues have also shown that under certain circumstances the opposite is true (Shiv et al. 2005b). In any event, these and other studies provide clear evidence that in normal health conditions our deliberative and decision-making processes are *always* informed by our affective states. All this seems to create a strong case against the traditional distinction between reason and passion.

According to the 'somatic marker hypothesis', formulated by Damasio at the beginning of the 1990s in explicit opposition to the idea that 'pure' logic and reason are our most effective decision-making tools, decision-making processes are influenced by the perception of bodily states that signal the value of the different options available to us. Somatic markers, which are acquired through experience and learning, emerge from the association of certain emotions and feelings with positive and negative events, and come into play during deliberation to 'qualify' the possible outcomes of our choices as either positive or negative:

> Somatic markers are thus acquired by experience, under the control of an internal preference system and under the influence of an external set of circumstances which include . . . social conventions and ethical rules. The neural basis for the internal preference system consists of mostly innate regulatory dispositions, posed to ensure survival of the organism. Achieving survival coincides with the ultimate reduction of unpleasant body states and the attaining of homeostatic ones, i.e., functionally balanced biological states. The internal preference system is inherently biased to avoid pain, seek potential pleasure, and is probably pretuned for achieving these goals in social situations. . . . The interaction between an internal preference system and sets of external circumstances extends the repertory of stimuli that will become automatically marked. (Damasio 1994: 179)

Somatic markers operate according to a twofold mechanism. The basic process consists in the body being engaged by the prefrontal cortex: it enters a specific state and the (visceral and musculoskeletal) characteristics of this change are transmitted to the somatosensory cortex. Alternatively, the somatosensory cortex can bypass the body and operate *as if* it had received the signal of a specific bodily state, so the brain will be able to foresee and anticipate bodily changes in order to enable quicker responses. In both cases, somatic markers can be activated without being made conscious.[1]

According to Damasio, the role of somatic markers is crucial especially when we face uncertain situations, as they streamline the decision-making process by picking the most promising options while letting the others recede into the background, thus reducing the level of complexity. Indeed, the somatic marker hypothesis was originally formulated as an attempt to explain decision-making deficits in patients with lesions of the ventromedial prefrontal cortex. Despite showing no signs of cognitive impairment, these patients seem unable to make advantageous choices (or even to choose at all, as they get stuck in an endless logical analysis of the possible alternatives). Consider for example the patient named EVR (Eslinger and Damasio 1985; 'Elliot' in Damasio 1994), who underwent bilateral ablation of the ventromedial frontal cortex to remove a meningioma at the age of thirty-five. Until then, EVR had lived a normal life: a married father of two, he worked as an accountant in a construction company and was respected by everyone. After surgery and a few months of convalescence, EVR went back to work and got involved in a business project with a rather shadowy figure. Oblivious to the warnings of friends and relatives who tried to discourage him, he invested his own capital and soon ended up losing everything. He then kept changing jobs and was repeatedly fired. His wife and children left him, so he had to go back to his parents. Two years after surgery, a follow-up check confirmed that EVR had successfully recovered from cancer. Except for bilateral anosmia, the neurological evaluation was positive and the patient's Wechsler Adult Intelligence Scale (WAIS) scores turned out to be average or above average. And yet EVR kept piling up an astonishing number of failures:

> For a while, he prepared income-tax returns, but was terminated. He then secured an accounting position in a firm located 100 miles from his house, but was fired for lack of punctuality. A month after his divorce, he remarried, against the advice of his relatives. That marriage ended in divorce 2 years later. He needed about 2 hours to get ready for work in the morning, and some days were consumed entirely by shaving and hair-washing. Deciding where to dine might take hours, as he discussed each restaurant's seating plan, particulars of menu, atmosphere, and management. He would drive to each restaurant to see how busy it was, but even then he could not finally decide which to choose. Purchasing small items required in-depth consideration of brands, prices, and the best method of purchase. He clung to outdated and useless possessions, refusing to part with dead houseplants, old phone books, six broken fans, five broken television sets, three bags of empty orange juice concentrate cans, 15 cigarette lighters, and countless stacks of old newspapers. (Eslinger and Damasio 1985: 1732)

His perceptual, motor, mnemonic, linguistic and learning abilities had remained unaltered. And he also scored very high in tests that assess the ability to come up with viable solutions to hypothetical social problems, to consider the consequences of one's actions, and to predict the social outcomes of certain events. Yet for all this, EVR was incapable of affectively perceiving his own interests and, therefore, of making (good) choices.

Damasio's idea is that lesions in the ventromedial prefrontal cortex, which performs the crucial task of matching the representation of bodily states (whether real or anticipated) with the various options available, undermine the decision-making capacity of the patient because they prevent the activation of the somatic marker system. Most of the empirical evidence in support of the somatic marker hypothesis comes from the results of the experiment known as the 'Iowa Gambling Task', which was first devised by Antoine Bechara, Hanna and Antonio Damasio and Steven Anderson in 1994 (Bechara et al. 1994).[2] In its basic version, the experiment involves a player who receives a loan of $2,000 in play money, and is asked to choose one card at a time from any of four identical decks. The game continues until the player is informed that the test is over. Each card chosen by the player corresponds to either a payoff or a penalty, the amount of which becomes known only after the card is turned over. The aim of the game is to maximize the profit starting from the initial sum. The player is unaware that the game will end when the hundredth card is drawn, and she is equally unaware (and cannot determine by calculation) that payoffs and penalties have been arranged according to the following scheme: each winning card in decks A and B always yields a payoff of $100, and each winning card in decks C and D always yields a payoff of $50; however, some cards in decks A and B are attached to substantial penalties (up to a maximum of $1,250 for every ten cards drawn). The cards in decks C and D are 'safer', resulting in far lower penalties (about $250 for every ten cards drawn). A comparison between the performance of healthy individuals and that of patients with lesions of the ventromedial prefrontal cortex revealed that the former show an initial preference for decks A and B, but then turn relatively quickly to decks C and D, securing a net profit of $250. The latter, by contrast, after testing all decks available, systematically insist on decks A and B; indeed, they go so far as to lose the entire starting sum halfway through the game. Interestingly, the patients with lesions of the ventromedial prefrontal cortex *do know* that decks A and B are riskier than decks C and D. Nonetheless, they carry on playing as if they were unaware of this. Why? At first, researchers came up with three possible explanations: (a) hypersensitivity to reward – the prospect of a future loss is always assigned less weight than the prospect of an immediate payoff; (b) insensitivity to punishment – the prospect of a payoff always prevails and (c) myopia for the future – insensitivity to any future consequence, whether positive or negative. After rearranging the game so as to invert the order of payoffs and penalties, researchers found that patients with lesions were still mostly influenced by the immediate results of their choices (this time: penalties) rather than by future prospects. If, as it appears to be the case, subjects of this kind tend to disregard long-term consequences, this is presumably due to their failure to activate somatic markers that should inform them of the disadvantages they risk facing. In 1996, Antoine Bechara and colleagues measured the skin conductance responses (SCRs) of the participants in the Iowa Gambling Task and classified them into three different categories: responses generated after selecting a winning card (reward SCRs), those generated after selecting a losing card (punishment SCRs) and those that were generated prior to the selection of any card (anticipatory SCRs). In patients with lesions of the ventromedial prefrontal cortex, changes in skin conductance were detected only as responses to the selection of a card. By contrast, healthy patients also showed anticipatory responses, with particularly high aSCRs values in response to 'risky' decks. Based on the correlation between absence of aSCRs and inability to make advantageous choices, researchers confirmed the hypothesis sketched in the previous study, concluding that

[patients with prefrontal lesions] have lost a critical system, centered in ventromedial prefrontal cortices, which normally (1) connects knowledge about the categorization of previous experiences, to different profiles of biological response including those that are part of an emotional response; and (2) has the ability to inhibit or activate the response appropriate to a given situation, by firing upon central bioregulatory structures such as those in the amygdalae and hypothalamus. (Bechara et al. 1996: 223)

From a neurobiological point of view, the somatic marker hypothesis is in line with psychological theories of decision-making processes that emphasize the importance of the idiosyncratic evaluation of the consequences of one's choices, in contrast with the criteria of classical rationality – as is the case, for example, with the so-called 'prospect theory' (Kahneman and Tversky 1979). Psychologists Daniel Kahneman and Amos Tversky famously criticized the accuracy of the theory of expected utility in descriptive psychology and proposed another account of what happens when we make decisions under conditions of risk. According to the theory of expected utility, decisions under conditions of risk are governed by the criterion of maximum utility, that is to say, they are based on a weighted average of the utility of each of the possible outcomes against their respective degree of probability. The theory of expected utility rests on an assumption of rationality understood as the fulfilment of some minimal requirements of systematicity and consistency such as, for example, transitivity (if X is preferred to Y and Y is preferred to Z, then X is preferred to Z), substitution (if X is preferred to Y, an even chance to obtain X or Z is preferred to an even chance to obtain Y or Z) and, in general, the principles of dominance and invariance. The principle of dominance holds that if X is as good as Y in every respect and better that X in one respect, then X must be chosen over Y. The principle of invariance holds that our preferences must not be affected by the way in which options are presented to us. Kahneman and Tversky argue that the theory of expected utility is unable to formulate accurate predictions of individual choices because the axioms on which it is based are in fact regularly violated. This claim draws on their analysis of the role of what, in a 1984 article entitled 'Choices, Values, and Frames', they called the 'psychophysics' of value (i.e. the attitude that, in the agent, induces risk aversion in the domain of gains and risk-seeking behaviour in the domain of losses), as well on their study on how subjective preferences can be influenced by changing the way in which the available options are presented and framed. Risk aversion is a particularly strong form of sensitivity to the losses we might incur, which also implies, conversely, an inclination to underestimate the potential gains we might obtain. Kahneman and Tversky turn to this psychological feature to criticize a key element of the theory of expected utility: when we make a decision or choice, we do not picture utility from the point of view of the final outcome of this decision or choice in terms of wealth or well-being, but rather from our own subjective point of view, as agents who can gain or lose something with respect to their current situation. We are thus more averse to losing X than we are attracted to gaining X_1, in the sense that, for example, we prefer a sure gain of 50 rather than participating in a lottery with an 85 per cent probability of winning 100 and a 15 per cent probability of winning nothing, even though mathematically speaking the lottery offers us better prospects (0.85 x 100 + 0.15 x 0 = 85). Conversely, if presented with the choice between a sure loss of 50 and an 85 per cent probability of losing 100 versus a 15 per cent probability of losing nothing, we will behave asymmetrically and choose to participate in the lottery (with an expected value of −85).

Risk aversion in the domain of gains and risk-seeking behaviour in the domain of losses underpin what is normally referred to as the 'framing effect', that is the bias where people decide on their preferences based on the way options are presented. Tversky and Kahneman (1981) illustrated this effect by presenting the following problem to a group of students at Stanford and British Columbia universities:

> Imagine that the U.S. is preparing for the outbreak of an unusual Asian disease, which is expected to kill 600 people. Two alternative programs to combat the disease have been proposed. Assume that the exact scientific estimates of the consequences of the programs are as follows:
>
> - If Program A is adopted, 200 people will be saved.
> - If Program B is adopted, there is 1/3 probability that 600 people will be saved, and 2/3 probability that no people will be saved.
>
> Which of the two programs would you favor?

The majority (72 per cent) of participants opted for programme A, considering the prospect of *certainly* saving 200 lives more attractive than running the risk of not saving anyone, thus showing *risk aversion*. Participants were then presented with another version of the same problem in which programmes A and B were replaced by the following options:

- If Program C is adopted 400 people will die.
- If Program D is adopted there is 1/3 probability that nobody will die, and 2/3 probability that 600 people will die.

In this case, the majority (78 per cent) of participants opted for programme D, as they considered the certain death of 400 people less acceptable than the 66.6 per cent probability that 600 people will die, thus displaying *risk-seeking* behaviour. Clearly, though, the two scenarios are in fact identical (A = C and B = D): the only difference is that the first group of options presents the outcomes in terms of lives saved, and the second in terms of lives lost. The inconsistency of the participants' preferences in Kahneman and Tversky's test is an emblematic case of violation of the principle of invariance presupposed by classical utility theory.

It has been observed that the somatic marker hypothesis is able to explain the phenomenon of risk aversion in the domain of gains and that of risk-seeking behaviour in the domain of losses on the basis of the neurobiological mechanism whereby information concerning highly probable outcomes stimulates a more intense somatic response than information concerning more remote probabilities (so that we prefer a smaller but sure gain to a larger but only probable one, and we fear a smaller but sure loss more than a larger but only probable one; see Bechara and Damasio 2005: 356).

In general, affective states seem to interfere significantly with the heuristic mechanisms that are relied upon when it comes to assessing different options, estimating probabilities and predicting values. In this regard, Paul Slovic and colleagues speak of affective heuristics:

> representations of objects and events in people's minds are tagged to varying degrees with affect. In the process of making a judgment or decision, people consult or refer to an 'affect pool' containing all the positive and negative tags consciously or unconsciously associated with the representations. . . . Using an overall, readily available affective impression can be far easier – more efficient – than weighing the pros and cons or retrieving from memory many relevant examples, especially when the required judgment or decision is complex or mental resources are limited. (Slovic et al. 2007: 1335–6)

A particularly telling example of the interaction between affective states and heuristic principles concerns the so-called 'availability bias', that is the tendency to consider as more important, representative or probable what is easier to recall (Tversky and Kahneman 1974: 1127–8). Several studies show how the perception of the seriousness and probability of a risk is inextricably linked to the intensity with which this risk arouses fear (e.g. Fischoff et al. 1978; Peters and Slovic 1996).[3]

In general, the heuristic mechanisms that we resort to in order to process beliefs and judgements are quite useful and allow us to greatly simplify the cognitive operations needed to find solutions, predict possibilities, calculate probabilities and so on. Damasio's studies on patients such as EVR demonstrate that somatic markers (or affective heuristics) are crucial to enabling advantageous choices. At the same time, however, there is evidence that those very same affective mechanisms may prevent us from noticing what the best options are. In 2005, for example, Baba Shiv and colleagues showed that patients with focal lesions in the brain areas involved in affective regulation are less myopically risk-averse than healthy subjects (Shiv et al. 2005b; see also Shiv et al. 2005a), thus substantiating the hypothesis (already put forward by Loewenstein et al. 2001: 273) that the phenomenon of myopic loss aversion, that is greater sensitivity to losses than to gains combined with a tendency to evaluate the outcome of one's investments very frequently (Benartzi and Thaler 1995), is rooted within the affective dimension of cognitive processes. Apparently, subjects who make judgements and decisions using a foreign language are also less exposed to the framing effect, and, in particular, to the phenomenon of myopic loss aversion. According to Keysar and colleagues, the use of a foreign language leads one to take a more affectively detached perspective compared to one's mother tongue (Keysar, Hayakawa and Sun Gyu 2012; see also Pavlenko 2012; Costa et al. 2014; Hayakawa et al. 2016; Ivaz, Costa and Duñabeitia 2016; Shin and Kim 2017). In sum, it seems reasonable to conclude that neural systems that subserve human emotions have evolved for survival purposes. The automatic emotions triggered by a given situation help the normal decision-making process by narrowing down the options for action, either by discarding those that are dangerous or endorsing those that are advantageous. Emotions serve an adaptive role speeding up the decision-making process. However, there are circumstances in which a naturally occurring emotional response must be inhibited, so that a deliberate and potentially wiser decision can be made. . . . Depending on the circumstances, moods and emotions can play useful as well as disruptive roles in the process of making advantageous decisions. (Shiv, Loewenstein and Bechara 2005a: 91)

Part III

Part III

Action

Dewey

The theory of emotion of American pragmatist philosopher John Dewey represents an important attempt to integrate Darwin's explanation of the origin and nature of emotions with the emphasis placed by James on the physiology of emotional experience. Dewey wrote two essays devoted to the critical reconstruction of Darwin's and James's positions, which were published in *Psychological Review* in 1894 and 1895, respectively: in the first, entitled 'The theory of emotion. (I) Emotional attitudes', Dewey analyses and revises the key ideas advanced by Darwin in *The Expression of the Emotions in Man and Animals*; in the second, entitled 'The theory of emotion. (II) The significance of emotions', he deals instead with what he calls the 'discharge theory', by which he means the theory of William James.

First, Dewey (1894) wants to dispel the misunderstanding that may result from Darwin's use of the term 'expression': for to classify the bodily changes that accompany emotions as *expressions*, that is as phenomena observed from the point of view of a spectator, is to commit what James (1890i: 196) had called the 'psychologist's fallacy' (Dewey 1894: 555). Of course, to an observer bodily manifestations of emotions are *signs*, but for the subject who is experiencing those emotions such manifestations are primarily actions, or functional modes of behaviour. As we have seen, Darwin himself essentially uses the term 'expressions' to indicate 'bodily changes', arguing that these have acquired a communicative function only secondarily, and that they should be primarily understood as types of behaviour, that is as actions (originally) conducive to maximizing survival chances. Dewey seems only partly aware of this.[1] On the one hand, he recognizes that according to the principle of serviceable associated habits expressions are to be understood as 'attitudes, . . . acts originally useful not qua expressing emotion, but qua acts – as serving life' (Dewey 1894: 555). On the other hand, he criticizes Darwin for framing the link between emotions and peripheral activity in terms of a linear sequence, in which the former precede and cause the latter:[2]

> the very phrase 'expression of emotion', as well as Darwin's method of stating the matter, begs the question of the relation of emotion to organic peripheral action, in that it assumes the former as prior and the latter as secondary. (Dewey 1894: 553)

The upshot of Dewey's functionalist characterization of emotions as actions is that emotion and expression are the same thing (i.e. an emotion is the same as the bodily changes that express it). On this basis, Dewey also challenges Darwin's principle of antithesis, according to which antithetical emotions correspond to opposite types of behaviour that may be devoid of a specific function – for even in such cases there must be an explanation rooted in the pragmatic utility of behaviour. Therefore, 'all so-called expressions of emotions are, in reality, the reduction of movements and stimulations originally useful into attitudes' (Dewey 1894: 568–9).

From a standpoint such as James's, which Dewey seeks to combine with Darwin's evolutionary naturalism, the idea that peripheral activity is secondary to the primary phenomenon of emotion is clearly unacceptable, since emotions *are* in fact the perception of bodily changes and behaviour. By reinterpreting the principle of serviceable associated habits in the light of the Jamesian hypothesis that 'the emotional "feel" is always due to the return wave of this attitude' (Dewey 1895: 14), Dewey states that

> Emotion in its entirety is a mode of behavior which is purposive, or has an intellectual content, and which also reflects itself into feeling or Affects, as the subjective valutation of that which is objectively expressed in the idea or purpose. (Dewey 1895: 15)

In an effort to spell out this preliminary definition in greater detail, Dewey (1895) embarks on a revision of James's theory, claiming that its main shortcoming lies in its failure 'to connect the emotional seizure with the other phases of the concrete emotion-experience. What the whole condition of *being* angry, or hopeful or sorry maybe, Mr. James nowhere says, nor does he indicate why or how the "feel" of anger related to them' (Dewey 1895: 16). In this sense, James's theory is about the feeling of emotions, and does not address emotions per se (and, Dewey claims, it is James himself who admits it when 'he expressly refers to his task as "subtracting certain *elements of feeling* from an emotional state supposed to exist *in its fulness*"', Dewey 1895: 15).

Dewey states that, in addition to feeling, there are at least two other aspects to consider: the first concerns behaviour, that is the pragmatic nature of emotion, with the actions it disposes one to perform; the second concerns the content of emotion, that is its intentional structure. Emotion

> is a disposition, a mode of conduct, a way of behaving. . . . Grief means *unwillingness* to resume the normal occupation, practical discouragement, breaking-up of the normal reactions, etc., etc. Just as anger means a tendency to explode in a sudden attack, not a mere state of feeling. (Dewey 1895: 16–7)

At the same time, emotion is always directed towards something, in the sense that it involves taking on a certain attitude towards what constitutes its "'object" or intellectual content' (Dewey 1895: 17). This is true, according to Dewey, also for those emotions that James defines as 'pathological' *qua* (apparently) devoid of any object. In fact, even in cases of this kind there is an intentional coordination between the bodily changes typical of the emotion and at least the possibility of an object. We can find evidence of this in the fact that people suffering from depression, anxiety, or exaltation often tend to identify the content of their feeling *ex post*: 'This feeling of depression must have its reason; the world is dark and gloomy; no one understands me; . . . This feeling of buoyancy must have its ideal reference; I am a delightful person, or one of the elect or have had a million dollars left me' (Dewey 1895: 18). The intentional structure is also what makes it possible to distinguish emotions from 'idiopathic discharges' (e.g. shivers of fear from shivers of cold), thus accounting once again for the functional nature of emotional behaviour (Dewey 1894: 561–2).

The connection between emotion and intentional object should not, however, be understood as a relation between distinct entities: the content is 'an integral phase of the single pulse of emotion; for emotion, as well as the idea, comes as a whole carrying its distinctions of value within it' (Dewey 1895: 17). If emotion arose from the conscious apprehension of a particular object, then such an object would need to be the object of that emotion even before it is apprehended. If tachycardia, shivering and running away from an object depended on an explicit and conscious intellectual operation through which we have recognized that object as a bear, then this would necessarily be a bear that we were already afraid of, and which we now recognize as a *frightening bear* (see Dewey 1895: 19). To put it differently, if emotion were nothing more than a reaction to a stimulus, then the stimulus would have to possess in itself, quite independently of us, the specific axiological properties of that particular emotion. But for Dewey this is not the case:

It is not the idea of the bear, or the bear as object, but a certain *act of seeing*, which by habit, whether inherited or acquired, sets up other acts. It is the kind of *coordination of acts* which, brought to sensational consciousness, constitutes the bear a fearful or a laughable or an indifferent object. . . . The idea or object which precedes and stimulates the bodily discharge is in no sense the idea or object (the intellectual content, the 'at' or 'on account of') of the emotion itself. The particular idea, the specific quality or object to which the seizure attaches, is just as much due to the discharge as is the seizure itself. . . . the idea or the object is an abstraction from the activity . . . (Dewey 1895: 19–20)

The perception of the bear (namely 'the act of seeing') is already affectively loaded. The relevant axiological properties of a given emotional experience *emerge* from the emotional experience itself, to wit, from the organism-environment relation that, following a naturalistic and functionalist approach, Dewey describes in terms of behaviour:

The reaction is not made on the basis of the apprehension of some quality in the object; it is made on the bases of an organized habit, of an organized coordination of activities, one of which instinctively stimulates the other. The outcome of this coordination of activities constitutes, for the first time the object with such and such an import – terrible, delightful, etc. – or constitutes an emotion referring to such as such an object. For, we must insist once more, the frightful object and the emotion of fear are two names for the same experience. (Dewey 1895: 20)

In other words, the object that elicits the emotion exists as such by virtue of the organism's behaviour and action possibilities: its *affective value* depends on the way the organism interacts or can interact with it. This value is expressed in the alterations and behaviour which, to the extent that they are experienced, constitute the feeling of the emotion. For Dewey, therefore, the analytic distinction between perceptual and ideational as well as between sensory and motor aspects of the emotional process is nothing but an abstraction, which should not be transferred from the level of reflection to the level of experience, for here

> we have but the one organic pulse, the frightful bear, the frightened man, whose reality is the whole concrete coordination of eye–leg–heart, &c., activity, and . . . the distinction of cold intellectuality and warm emotionality is simply a *functional* distinction within this one whole of action. We take a certain phase which *serves a certain end*, namely, giving us information, and call that intellectual; we take another phase, having another end or value, that of excitement, and call that emotional. But does any one suppose that, *apart from our interpretation of values*, there is one process in itself intellectual, and another process in itself emotional? (Dewey 1895: 21)

The idea that perceptions, thoughts, feelings and behaviour are distinct phases that follow one another in a linear sequence is replaced with the notion of 'coordination'. In doing so, Dewey paves the way for the concept of 'organic circuit', which he will soon exploit to criticize the concept of reflex arc in psychology, as well as stimulus–response dualism (Dewey 1896): sensorimotor coordination consists in a dynamic interaction between organism and environment in which the former contributes to selecting stimuli and outlining their relevant features, while the latter sets the conditions of possibility for the behaviour of the organism, along with specific limits and constraints. In conclusion, an emotion and its intentional object are reciprocally defined: outside of the domain of analytic considerations, there is no linear causal sequence between stimulation and response from the organism.

Within the framework of this dynamic scheme, Dewey describes 'emotional seizure' as the awareness of an adaptive effort, of a tension in the coordination between perceptual and conceptual behaviour on the one hand, and autonomic and motor behaviour on the other hand. When the functional unity of coordination is harmonious, then behaviour unfolds smoothly; conversely, emotions set in when a given habit is inhibited:

> The attitude is precisely that which was a complete activity once, but is no longer so. The activity of seizing prey or attacking an enemy, a movement having its meaning in itself, is now reduced or aborted; it is an attitude simply. As an instinctive reaction it is thoroughly ingrained in the system; it represents the actual coordinations of thousands and thousands of ancestors; it tends to start into action, therefore whenever its associated stimulus occurs. But the very fact that it is now reduced to an attitude or tendency, the very fact that is now relatively easy to learn to control the instinctive blind reaction when we are stimulated in a certain way, shows that the primary activity is inhibited; it no longer exists as a whole by itself, but simply as a coordinated phase, or a contributory means, in a larger activity. (Dewey 1895: 27–8)

It is in this coordination breakdown that the functional distinction between stimulus and behavioural response emerges, together with the intentional structure of emotion, which thus constitutes a phase of the unity of coordination, of the functional interaction between organism and environment.

Dewey's legacy plays a major role in contemporary debate, especially in the form of a critique of body–mind dualism, along with the inner–outer, stimulus–response and feeling–action divides. The analysis of emotions and actions as mutually dependent variables and the emphasis on the interaction between behaviour and the evaluation of stimuli have proved to be crucial tools for problematizing the classical 'sandwich model' of the mind (Hurley 1998, 2001). According to this model, perception and action are independent and peripheral processes separated from cognitive activity (just as in a sandwich the slices of bread are distinct from the filling), whereby the latter plays the crucial role of processing information in amodal language (i.e. independently of sensory modes) and sending the signals required to generate behavioural responses. In this sense, Dewey's philosophy is an important source of inspiration for the enactivist approach and for the pragmatist turn in the new cognitive sciences (see below, pp. 134–44). Before turning to the enactivist programme, however, we shall take a broader look at the contemporary debate in general, and especially at the work of Nico Frijda, which sparked considerable interest in the link between emotion and action. Finally, it is worth noting that, in philosophical debate, action tendencies emerge as the constitutive dimension of emotional phenomena especially in Julien Deonna and Fabrice Teroni's attitudinal theory, as well as in Andrea Scarantino's motivational theory.

Emotions as action tendencies

In contemporary research, a compelling analysis of the relation between emotions and actions comes from Dutch psychologist Nico Frijda (1986, 2007 and 2010). Frijda describes the 'emotional process' (namely the process that occurs between stimulus and response) in cognitivist terms: first of all, the subject registers a stimulus (which can be a physical or mental event, such as a thought, ideation or imagining) and evaluates it in relation to her own interests and needs. This essentially amounts to Lazarus's primary appraisal (see above, pp. 85–6). Next, the subject considers the eliciting stimulus in relation to the situation in which it occurs, and assesses to what extent she is able to cope with the problem or exploit the opportunity she is presented with (as Lazarus himself envisaged with the notion of secondary appraisal: see above, pp. 86–8). At the same time, the subject's action priorities (or 'control precedence') are revised based on the context-specific degree of seriousness, difficulty, urgency etc. For instance, upon receiving a stimulus the subject may quit the activity she was performing, while her attention is diverted away from goals and feelings that are not immediately relevant. This leads to a change in 'action readiness', as a certain course of action acquires 'control precedence' over others. As the physiological conditions conducive to such behavioural priority are brought about, the relevant action is selected (Frijda 1986: 454–6).

Although Frijda explicitly acknowledges that his approach owes much to the cognitivist tradition of appraisal theory, he prefers to qualify his theory as *conative*. On his view emotions essentially are changes in 'action readiness' that differ from each other quantitatively (i.e. on the basis of the degree of arousal they bring about), qualitatively (i.e. on the basis of the type of action tendencies they promote) and autonomically (i.e. on the basis of the different physiological changes that accompany them). The notion of 'action tendencies', which Frijda retrieves from Arnold (1960) and turns into the key tenet of his whole theory, refers in his view to inclinations to bring about certain types of behaviour that display a characteristic urgency ('control precedence'):

> Action tendencies have the character of urges or impulses. Action tendencies . . . clamor for attention and for execution. They lie in waiting for signs that they can or may be executed; they, and their execution, tend to persist in the face of interruptions;

they tend to interrupt other ongoing programs and actions; and
they tend to preempt the information-processing facilities. . . .
Evidently, then, action tendencies are programs that have a
place of precedence in the control of action and of information
processing. . . . Action tendencies – action readiness changes
generally – have the feature of *control precedence*. (Frijda 1986:
78)

More specifically, action tendencies are states of 'readiness' to
perform a given action that must be defined based on the action's
goal (see Frijda 1986: 70). Accordingly, an action tendency consists in
the readiness to perform different types of actions that share the same
goal. This, in turn, makes it possible to account for the behavioural
flexibility typical of emotional reactions. For example, the action
tendency associated with anger may be expressed by attacking,
insulting or storming off, depending on which behaviour is possible
or appropriate in a given context. Still, all these types of behaviour
share the same goal, namely getting rid of the obstacle, taking power
or control back, or, more generally, taking revenge. However, there are
emotions that do not seem to be directed towards the achievement of
any goal: this is the case, for example, of what Frijda calls 'relational
null states', such as disinterest or passive sadness. In these cases,
the desire or willingness to act is reduced or absent altogether, and
seemingly devoid of any goal that could define it. Some forms of joy
raise the same problem: they lack, in whole or in part, a specific goal
that qualifies the corresponding action tendency. Frijda tries to solve
this problem by introducing the notion of 'action readiness as such',
which should account both for the depotentiation of the readiness to
act (e.g. in cases of apathetic depression) and for the manifestation
of generalized readiness (e.g. in cases of joyful excitement). In these
cases, too, we are dealing with reactions to stimuli or events that are

significant for the subject and with processes that change the state of readiness to act:

> *Emotions, then, can be defined as modes of relational action readiness, either in the form of tendencies to establish, maintain, or disrupt a relationship with the environment or in the form of mode of relational readiness as such.* (Frijda 1986: 71)

Finally, Frijda's view on subjective phenomenology draws on Arnold, who describes emotions as 'action tendencies, felt impulses to action' (Arnold 1960: 194), and defines emotion as 'awareness of action tendency – of desire to strike or to flee, to investigate or to be with' (Frijda 1986: 71). Subjective emotional experience is therefore nothing more than the feeling of a certain action tendency.

The attitudinal theory of emotions

Especially from the 1960s onwards, the nature of the link between emotions and values has become an increasingly pressing issue, which has given rise to a number of related theories (see above, pp. 79–102). Indeed, the prospect of illustrating emotions in terms of the values to which they refer (where 'values' is taken to mean, in a neutral sense, the axiological properties instantiated by the particular objects of emotion) exerts a strong appeal both at the level of ordinary intuitions and at a more distinctively theoretical level. In particular, as we have seen in greater detail in Part II (see above, pp. 79–83), the reference to values seems to allow for the identification of different kinds of emotions (all cases of fear have to do with danger, all cases of anger have to do with offence and so on), their intelligibility ('[it] is not possible . . . to envy something which one believes to belong to oneself, or to feel remorse for something in which one believes one had no part', Kenny 1963: 135) and their appropriateness (does the particular object of my emotion of fear really exemplify its relevant axiological property?).

With their attitudinal theory, Julien Deonna and Fabrice Teroni (2012, 2014 2015) aim to account for the intentional relation between emotions and axiological properties; unlike traditional evaluative approaches, however, they do so by locating this relation not at the level of the content of emotions, but rather at the level of psychological attitude. Deonna and Teroni (2012, 2015) start from the distinction, common in philosophy of mind, between psychological *content* and *attitude*, that is between what the mind addresses and the 'way' in which it addresses it. The rationale of this distinction lies in the fact that the same psychological attitude can have different contents (for instance, I may believe that women's rights are human rights, that there is a vase of flowers on my desk, that I am going to eat pizza tonight, etc.), whereas, conversely, different psychological attitudes may share the same content (for instance, I may think that it is going to rain, or hope that it will rain, or suppose that it is about to rain). Evaluative theories that identify emotions with value judgements (e.g. Solomon [1976] 1993), equate them with perceptions of value (e.g. Tappolet 2016), or describe them as combinations of beliefs and desires (e.g. Searle 1983), rest on the assumption that the psychological attitude is always the same (whether a judgement, a perception or a combination of beliefs and desires). This in turn entails that the axiological dimension of emotional experience lies in its content: to be angry is to ascertain, perceive or believe that one has been wronged, and to long for revenge; to be afraid is to ascertain, perceive, or believe that something is dangerous, and to long for safety and so on. Deonna and Teroni resist this view, claiming that emotions consist of particular psychological attitudes of an evaluative nature. It is worth stressing that, on this view, experiencing an emotion does not mean adopting the 'the attitude of *emoting*' with regard to a given content – for if this were the case, then we would once again be faced with the problematic task of having to tell emotions apart on the basis of the quality of their content. The idea here is rather that there are as many emotional attitudes as there are emotions. This type of approach has a number of advantages. First, it enables us to account for the fact that different attitudes may share the same content. Any evaluative content is compatible with more than one attitude, whether emotional or otherwise: for instance, we can certainly be afraid of something dangerous, but we can also be disappointed or surprised by it; we can imagine it, wonder about it and so on. Therefore, an emotion is characterized by the axiological quality of our relation with its content, and not by the content itself. In addition, the attitudinal theory imposes no restrictions on the type of content towards which an emotion can be directed. Whereas emotions have necessarily a propositional content if understood as value judgements and a non-propositional content if they are described as perceptions of value, by qualifying each emotion in terms of its specific attitude we can maintain that emotions can have both a propositional content (e.g. when one regrets that the meat is rotten) and a non-propositional one (e.g. when one is disgusted by the rotten meat). This is so because emotions derive their content from different psychological states (e.g. we can feel tenderness for a child whom we *watch* playing, whom we *remember* playing, whom *we imagine* playing, etc.), of which they retain the typological quality (which, again, can be either propositional or non-propositional).

It is at the phenomenological level that the attitudinal theory emphasizes the relation between emotions and action tendencies. Deonna and Teroni appeal to William James's observations on the centrality of the perception of bodily changes in emotional experience, which they combine with Peter Goldie's insights on 'feeling towards'

(Goldie 2000; see above, pp. 95–7) in order to account for the fact that emotions can be directed towards something beyond one's own body. Against this background, the bodily experience typical of emotional episodes is couched in terms of a subjective attitude that involves a specific feeling of one's body but is directed towards something that goes beyond it. More specifically, Deonna and Teroni take from Nico Frijda the notion of 'action readiness' and maintain that

> emotions are evaluative attitudes because they are bodily experiences of being disposed or tending to act in a differentiated way vis-à-vis a given object or event. The relevant notion of felt bodily attitude should be broad enough to encompass the felt readiness to move away, towards or against a given object, to contemplate it, to submit to it, to be attracted by it, to disengage from it or even to suspend any kind of interaction with it. In fear, one feels one's own body poised to defuse something; in anger, one feels its preparedness to deal with it in an actively hostile way; in shame, one feels one's readiness to escape from the look of those who make one feel ashamed; and in sadness, one feels one's body go weak as it is deprived of any interaction with the absent object whose qualities we are actively attending to. (Deonna and Teroni 2015: 302–3)

However useful it may be to account for the various contents to which the same attitude can be directed, and, conversely, for the various attitudes that can be directed to the same contents, it is not entirely clear to what extent the distinction between *attitude* and *content* is cognitively and phenomenologically accurate. Deonna and Teroni concede that at the level of experience emotions have a unitary and homogeneous character while attitudes and content are abstractions, but nevertheless argue that the latter function as 'independent variables' (Deonna and Teroni 2015: 305). In this sense, Deonna and Teroni seem rather distant from the Deweyan idea of an organic circuit: to the extent that it does not offer an analysis of the interaction and co-constitution of psychological attitudes and of their contents, attitudinal theory reiterates the separation of subject and object, inner and outer, organism and environment.

The motivational theory of emotions

The motivational theory developed by Andrea Scarantino (2014, 2017) explicitly aims to assign proper weight to the role played by emotions in causing behaviour: evaluative processes remain core aspects of emotional experience, as does the phenomenological dimension of emotional experience (i.e. the way it feels), and yet they have no bearing on its definition. In this sense, Scarantino distances himself both from cognitivist accounts and from perceptualist interpretations, while he is much more sympathetic to Nico Frijda's reflections on 'action tendencies' and on the urgency ('control precedence') they display (see above, pp. 124–7).

To substantiate his concerns about cognitivism and perceptualism, which in his view are unable to account for the motivational dimension of emotions, Scarantino (2014) targets the so-called 'mixed' theories of the cognitivist tradition, which regard emotions as a combination of beliefs and desires, while he levels his critique of perceptualism against Jesse Prinz's view. For mixed theories, emotions consist of evaluative beliefs, which record what Lazarus has termed 'core relational themes' (see above, p. 87), along with the corresponding desires: for example, fear consists in the belief that something is dangerous, coupled with the desire to avoid the danger; anger consists in the belief that one has been wronged, coupled with the desire to take revenge and so on. Scarantino points out that the combination of beliefs and desires is neither necessary nor sufficient to explain the phenomenon of emotional motivation. On the one hand, it is perfectly possible, and indeed relatively frequent, that one is inclined to a certain kind of behaviour even in the absence of a corresponding evaluative belief (or in the presence of an evaluative belief that even justifies the opposite behaviour): this is the case of phobias and, in general, of the so-called 'recalcitrant emotions' (see pp. 92–3 above). Moreover, if we held that the motivation to act depended on forming a belief and a desire and on combining them by inference, we would have a hard time accounting for sudden behavioural responses and impulsive actions. On the other hand, it is possible to form an evaluative belief (e.g. 'this wild beast is dangerous') and to conceive the corresponding desire (e.g. to escape from danger) without engaging in the behaviour featuring the qualities that, according to Scarantino, characterize emotional motivation, namely impulsivity, flexibility and bodily underpinnings (Scarantino 2014: 157–60). There are different reasons why not even the theories that rely on an analogy between emotions and perceptions manage to shed light on the phenomenon of emotional motivation. According to Jesse Prinz, for example, emotion impels action only in an indirect manner, in the sense that while it does provide a 'motive' to act, it does not necessarily yield a 'motivation' to act. The hedonic quality or 'valence marker' of an emotion is not associated to its object, but rather to the emotion itself *qua* somatic state: positive hedonic valence markers suggest selecting actions that sustain a somatic state; negative valence markers suggest making a change (Prinz 2004a: 191–6, 228–9). According to Scarantino, an approach that on a pragmatic level uncouples the goal of behaviour from the context of interaction with the stimulus and conceives the former as relating directly only to the organism's internal state, has the advantage of providing a flexible picture of behavioural responses (e.g. the goal of altering one's somatic state of fear in the face of danger is compatible both with the attempt to run away and with that to attack and destroy the enemy), but overall ushers in quite unrealistic implications. If fear, instead of urging us to avoid danger, primarily led us to change our somatic state, then escaping from the danger, trying not to think about it or taking a tranquillizer would be equally valid strategies.

For Scarantino, emotions directly trigger the relevant action tendencies (Scarantino 2017: 331–2). Emotions are therefore 'behavioral programs' defined by reference to their function, which is to direct behaviour through the selective potentiation of coherent sets of behavioural options (Scarantino 2014, 2017). Thus, fear is essentially the selective potentiation of actions aimed at avoiding danger; anger is essentially the selective potentiation of actions aimed at getting rid of an obstacle or reacting to an offence, and so on. In other words, emotions are behavioural control programmes prompted by a core relational theme that serve the function of ranking certain goals over others. This mechanism for ranking some action tendencies over others can be aptly illustrated with the notion of 'control precedence' introduced by Nico Frijda (1986). When an emotional action tendency takes priority over others, it interrupts competing processes that are not geared to satisfying the goals promoted by the emotion, nor to preparing the body for action (so that for instance information and inputs that are not immediately useful are locked out, as when fear temporarily inhibits the perception of hunger, pain or other inputs that would risk diverting the organism from its real priority, that is the task of escaping from the danger). The definition upon which the motivational theory is based is therefore the following:

An emotion is a prioritizing action control system, expressed either by (in)action tendencies with control precedence or by action reflexes, with the function of achieving a certain relational goal while correlating with a certain core relational theme. (Scarantino 2014: 178)

The enactivist revolution

In the field of the cognitive sciences, there are two main approaches to the investigation of the human mind. Lakoff and Johnson (1999) distinguish between first- and second-generation cognitive sciences. Alternatively, since the differences here are philosophical and methodological rather than chronological, it may be useful to distinguish between 'disembodied' and 'embodied' cognitive sciences. The core claims of classical (disembodied) cognitivism are based on the 'mind as computer' metaphor: the idea is that the mind is a sort of software that can be run on any kind of appropriate support and that, consequently, the hardware does not contribute in any way to determining the nature of the programmes that are run on it. Crucially, this leads to a strongly disembodied view of the mind. Dominant versions of computational and representational theories define cognition as the processing of mental representations, that is symbolic structures that have a propositional form (e.g. Fodor 1975, 1981, 2008). As exemplified by another metaphor, that of the 'sandwich model' of the mind (see above, p. 124), cognition consists in mediating between sensory inputs (perception) and motor outputs (action). Representationalism is coupled with an internalist assumption that locates mental representations in the mind (physically located in the brain), and regards them as separate from and independent of the external environment. The ontological and epistemological commitments of classical cognitivism can be summarized as follows: '(1) the world is pregiven; (2) our cognition is of this world – even if only to a partial extent, and (3) the way in which we cognize this pregiven world is to represent its features and then act on the basis of these representations' (Varela, Thompson and Rosch 1991: 135). The representational account of cognition quite naturally carries an 'objectivist' stance in its train, based on the assumption that the world

> consists of objects that have properties and stand in various relationships independent of human understanding. The world is as it is, no matter what any person happens to believe about it, and there is one correct 'God's-Eye-View' about what the world is really like. In other words, there is a rational structure to reality, independent of the beliefs of any particular people, and correct reason mirrors this rational structure. (Johnson 1987: x)

On this view external objects and their properties are as they are and the mind mirrors them, retrieving and organizing them in amodal, clearly defined categories whose correspondence with the external world constitutes the basic criterion for truth.

This model of the mind has been seriously challenged by philosophers and cognitive scientists working within the framework of 4E (embodied, embedded, extended and enacted) cognition. This approach fans out in several variants, which are often very different from each other. Despite their differences, however, they all work with notions of mindedness that go beyond the brain as a kind of computer, that is that cognitive processes are informed by the biological, physiological and morphological characteristics of the organism (*embodiment*), by the natural, social, and technological environment in which the organism is situated (*embeddedness* and *extension*) and by the organism's own interaction with the environment (*enaction*). Although they are different from each other in several respects, all the approaches in second-generation cognitive science converge on rejecting all forms of dualism implied by classical cognitivism. Cognition cannot be understood unless we jettison the dichotomy between mind and body, inner and outer as well as perception and action, thus appreciating the extent to which it is rooted in the body as a whole (as opposed to simply the head), dependent on extracorporeal processes and structures (including technological tools and cultural and social norms) and resulting from the active engagement of the organism with the external environment. According to the hypothesis of embodied cognition, cognitive processes are influenced (or even constituted) by non-neural bodily factors. The analysis of the role of the body in the production of meaning lies at the heart of several research projects, including for example the study of concept formation (Lakoff and Johnson 1980; see above, pp. 10–14) and that of bodily affects (e.g. hunger, fatigue, etc.) as prenoetic constraints on perceptual experience (Gallagher 2005). Cognitive activity also depends on the bodily exploitation of environmental structures and scaffolds: the hypothesis of embedded cognition explores 'the process by which animals build physical structures that transform problem spaces in ways that aid (or sometimes impede) thinking and reasoning about some target domain or domains' (Clark 2008: 62). For example, an experienced bartender will arrange glasses of different shapes in a spatial sequence that corresponds to the temporal sequence in which she received the drinks orders, so that the task of remembering the temporal sequence of the orders is turned into that of perceiving the different shapes of the glasses and associating them with the corresponding cocktails (Beach 1988). When in cases of this kind we rely on an external support to optimize our cognitive performance, do our psychological processes remain within the mind-body system or do they reach beyond its boundaries? According to the hypothesis of extended cognition, the external resources and their manipulation (e.g. the pen and paper we are using to do the maths or the mobile phone to which we have entrusted the 'memory' of our contacts) are in their own right part of the cognitive process, which as such consists of different components distributed across brain, body and external environment (Clark and Chalmers 1998). Finally, the enactivist project, initiated in 1991 with the publication of *The Embodied Mind* (Varela, Thompson and Rosch 1991), aims to integrate a phenomenological approach with a biological one that understands cognition in terms of a dynamic relationship between the organism and the environment geared to sustaining the organism's biological viability. The key ideas spurred by enactivism concern in particular the active role of the organism in the environment, which is not simply 'registered', but rather 'enacted'. Perception is for action (see above, p. 99), and cognition, distributed across brain, body and environment, amounts to an embodied and evaluative exploration of the world. The enactivist project has been developed in three main strands, respectively branded 'autopoietic' (e.g. Noë 2004), 'sensorimotor' (e.g. Varela, Thompson and Rosch 1991; Di Paolo 2005; Thompson 2007) and 'radical' enactivism (Hutto and Myin 2013; 2017). The autopoietic approach, in particular, endorses the view that cognition is a process of sense-making by an adaptively autonomous system, that is by an organism capable of altering its behaviour in response to environmental changes in order to optimize its conditions. Insofar as it emerges from the behaviour of an organism that seeks to either pursue or avoid given environmental features, cognition is inherently affective. From an enactivist perspective, affectivity represents the capacity of an organism to *care about* something, and is a phenomenon that is inherent in all forms of life. It cannot be detached from cognition: rather, it pervades it, informing and orienting not only 'basic' cognitive processes (such as sense perception), but also the so-called 'higher-order' processes, such as thinking, believing and judging.

In emotion theory, the dominant views are clearly under the sway of classical cognitivism: aside from the significant differences between evaluative and neo-Jamesian approaches, the dualism underlying classical cognitivism resurfaces as a pervasive trait of virtually every variant of these theories. Emotions are typically regarded as internal processes or states of the organism that are independent of the environment, whose role is limited to the generation of stimuli. The most radical proposals within the appraisal tradition interpret physical symptoms as side effects of abstract, intellectual cognitive processes. Even the theories that aim to cast light on the bodily dimension of emotions cannot resist the temptation to combine mental and physical processes as separate and distinct components. Within the framework of classical cognitivism, the most interesting attempt to reconcile the opposite poles of the body–mind dualism is probably that of Jesse Prinz, who claims that 'in developing a theory of emotion, we should not feel compelled to supplement embodied states with meaningful thoughts: we should instead put meaning into our bodies and let perceptions of the heart reveal our situation in the world' (Prinz 2004b: 58). As we have seen, however, Prinz maintains that an emotion is 'both an internal body monitor and a detector of dangers, threats, losses, or other matters of concern' (Prinz 2004a: 69), and defines it as the perception of bodily changes that represent axiological properties (the so-called 'core relational themes') that are independent of the organism. The idea that core relational themes exist objectively and independently of the cognitive activity of the organism, together with the implication that emotions represent them more or less correctly depending on whether the emotion-specific axiological property is instantiated by the particular object of the emotion, has attracted much criticism from scholars who subscribe to the so-called 4E approach, especially in its enactivist variant (e.g. Colombetti and Thompson 2008; Hutto 2012).

A core tenet of enactivism concerns the co-constitutive relation between cognition and its objects: the organism does not cognitively represent an external, objective reality; rather, by acting and interacting with the environment it brings forth features that are significant in relation to the organism itself, its biological and morphological structure, its bodily states and physiological needs, and so on. In this sense, emotions are not understood as the outcome of internal processes, but rather as dynamic products of the interaction between multiple brain, physical and environmental processes that influence each other. In response to the enactivist challenge, Prinz has recently revised his own view (Schargel and Prinz 2017) by wedding the notion of 'affordances' to the idea that the axiological meaning of emotion depends on the interaction between organism and environment (and not on the representation of the environment as is, that is independently of the organism). The notion of affordance was introduced in the field of ecological psychology by James Gibson with the aim of describing organism and environment as inseparable and complementary:

The *affordances* of the environment are what it *offers* the animal, what it *provides* or *furnishes*, either for good or ill. . . . I mean by it [the noun affordance] something that refers to both the environment and the animal in a way that no existing term does. It implies the complementarity of the animal and the environment. . . . An important fact about the affordances of the environment is that they are in a sense objective, real, and physical, unlike values and meanings, which are often supposed to be subjective, phenomenal, and mental. But, actually, an affordance is neither an objective property nor a subjective property; or it is both if you like. An affordance cuts across the dichotomy of subjective-objective and helps us to understand its inadequacy. (Gibson 1979: 127–9)

An affordance is an action possibility commensurate to the organism that perceives it. The same physical space provides different affordances for different life forms, as the abilities, the interests and the physical structure itself of the organism contribute to defining the properties of the environment. Water affords swimming to dolphins and walking to water striders (Gerridae); a leaf affords pulling to a worm and collecting to a human being who is compiling a herbarium; a woollen jumper affords eating to a moth and wearing to me and so on. Affordances are therefore the product of the interaction between the action possibilities and the aims of the organism, on the one hand, and the physical (but also cultural and social) characteristics of its environment, on the other hand. The idea that emotions represent affordances has been developed by Paul Griffiths and Andrea Scarantino (Griffiths and Scarantino 2009). In a 2009 paper entitled 'Emotions in the Wild: The Situated Perspective on Emotion', Griffiths and Scarantino argue that emotions should not be regarded primarily as more or less accurate responses to the state of things, but first and foremost as reactions that are more or less conducive to achieving a given goal. For this reason, their content should be interpreted pragmatically:

> imagine the world-as-perceived (*Umwelt*) of an antelope suddenly confronted by a lion. The dominant elements of the antelope's *Umwelt* are 'escape affordances' ..., as all of its cognitive, perceptual, and motoric abilities are recruited to discover and execute an action sequence that evades the predator. This representation of the world in goal-oriented terms is required by the urgency of the situation, which demands selectively transforming inputs into opportunities for life-saving output rather than generating a multipurpose representation of the environment. (Griffiths and Scarantino 2009: 441)

On this view, fear does not represent a danger, but rather affordances to escape from a danger. Moreover, the expressive and behavioural forms that emotion can take vary dynamically within the context of social interaction. Depending on the kind of feedback we receive from the subject with whom we interact (e.g. during a fight), we can pick up the affordance (e.g. retaliation if we are angry) in different ways (e.g. by pouting, insulting or storming off). Schargel and Prinz (2017) present the theory of emotions as affordances in a non-representationalist fashion, stating that emotions, by virtue of their bodily nature, do not merely pick up affordances from the environment, but rather create new opportunities for action:

> The embodiment of an emotion makes new actions possible because it places the body into a configuration where it can perform certain actions more easily than it could have before. One might think this is just a quantitative difference: emotions make action easier. We think it is more than that. Prior to an emotion, there is a sense in which any action compatible with our physical constitution is possible. So that claim that a given action could take place is, to that degree, trivial. When an action is potentiated by an actual bodily change, certain courses of action go from being mere possibilities to being something akin to dynamic attractors. Epistemically, a potentiated action becomes a salient option, and, motivationally, a potentiated action has a kind of command over it. (Schargel and Prinz 2017: 119)

Emotional affordances thus emerge only with the onset of emotion, and in this sense they are different from Gibsonian affordances, whose presence in the environment does not depend on the organism perceiving them (e.g. the door handle affords grabbing and turning even when I am not attending to it because I am busy writing this book at my desk). It is in these terms that Schargel and Prinz explain the motivational drive typical of emotion: Gibsonian affordances entail the possibility of a certain action, while emotional affordances demand it. Consequently,

> Anger does not pick up on the action that was demanded by the offense, but rather creates the demand; it temporarily transforms those who provoked anger, and potentially innocent others whom one happens to encounter while angry, into potential targets of aggression. Expression signals this, and action potentiation motivates it, thus creating new social relations that were not in place before the emotion. (Schargel and Prinz 2017: 122)

In conclusion, while the theory of embodied appraisal holds that emotions represent emotion-independent axiological properties (Prinz 2004a), its enactivist variant suggests that these properties emerge from the affectively loaded interaction between organism and environment.

Another enactivist revision of the theory of embodied appraisal has been put forward by Daniel Hutto (2012), who proposes replacing its teleosemantics with a teleosemiotic approach, thus relinquishing the idea that emotions are (more or less correct) representations of objective properties. From this point of view, according to Hutto, it is certainly the case that we are predisposed to be set off by core relational themes, to which we respond with forms of behaviour that involve the experience of bodily feelings; still, these behavioural forms ought to be understood as reactions to specific situations, and not as representations of the external world (see Hutto 2012: 179). An emotional response is thus an activity of the organism that interacts with its surrounding environment. This response has a 'felt' quality, which, however, is not a further component distinct from the response itself: the phenomenal character of experience is identical to the concrete activity of the organism capable of perception (see Hutto 2012: 181).

Within the enactivist approach, the most detailed analysis of the experiential dimension and evaluative nature of affective phenomena is undoubtedly that of Giovanna Colombetti (2014, 2018). For Colombetti, cognition and affectivity do not constitute two distinct systems, but are rather integrated at both the biological and psychological level. As far as emotions are concerned, their cognitive and evaluative dimension is itself embodied:

> the bodily processes you undergo when in the grip of jealousy are not mere contingent responses to essential, brain-bound cognitive evaluations; they are, rather, bodily ways of making sense of the situation, and as such they are cognitive-evaluative. Applied to appraisal theories in psychology, enactivism thus entails that appraisal ought not to be seen as a component of emotion distinct from other, bodily components with no cognitive-evaluative character. Rather, when we undergo an emotional episode, this is simultaneously bodily (it is a whole-organism process) and cognitive-evaluative (it is an evaluation of one's situation). Shaking, crying, etc., are bodily ways of evaluating the fact that one's partner has a lover as upsetting and threatening. Bodily changes are here parts of the material processes realizing a certain appraisal. (Colombetti 2018: 577)

Colombetti (2014) investigates the evaluative dimension of affective phenomena by fitting the latest neuroscientific evidence within the context of the phenomenological tradition. On the one hand, the distinction between the cognitive and the affective dimension of emotion does not seem backed by a corresponding functional organization of different brain areas (e.g. Lewis 2005; Pessoa 2008, 2010, 2013). On the other hand, the phenomenological analysis of emotional experience suggests that bodily feelings are themselves elements of the evaluation process. The idea is that the body should not be regarded as the object of our feelings, but rather as something through which we experience the world. Consequently, emotional feelings are not to be understood as feelings of the body, but as feelings of the world, which we affectively perceive through the experience of our body (Colombetti 2014: 106–9). Colombetti's approach clearly presupposes the rejection of an internalist perspective: cognition (including affective processes and emotions) consists in the ongoing exchange between organism and environment and can therefore extend beyond the boundaries of the organism, even in a physical sense. Within this framework, the extended affectivity hypothesis explores how material objects, artefacts and cultural and social institutions can become part of our affective experience, helping to structure it and to determine its development. In this regard, Colombetti (2016) discusses the phenomenon of 'affective object-incorporation', and does so by exploring in particular the subjective experience of musicians and the way in which playing music consorts with their affective states: just as we affectively perceive the world through the experience of our bodies, so the musician experiences her instrument as the medium through which a particular affective state emerges during the musical performance. Here, the instrument is not the intentional object of an emotion, nor is it merely integrated into the subject's sensorimotor schema as an actual sensory organ, as would be the case for instance with the cane for a blind person. During the musical performance, the instrument is an integral part also of the musician's affective experience, as it contributes significantly to playing it out. The hypothesis of affective incorporation thus sheds light on how we organize and regulate our affective experience by manipulating space, tools and, in general, the physical, cultural and social environment that surrounds us.

Debate III
Emotions towards fictional characters[1]

'A certain experience of its [sc. the soul's] own': with these words, Gorgias alludes to the feelings of those who, upon hearing the poetic account of the success and misfortunes of others, are struck by 'fearful shuddering, tearful pity, and a longing that loves to lament' (DK 82 B 11: 9). In the ancient world, fear and pity are the emotions par excellence that characterize the audience's response to tragic representations. Similar emotions are also described by Hamlet when, stunned by the power of the dramatic effect, he sees the actor's face turning pale, his eyes filling with tears and his voice trembling as he recites in verse Hecuba's despair at the sight of the brutal murder of her husband. What most strikes Hamlet, however, is not the intensity of the passion that overwhelms the actor, but rather its cause or, more precisely, its unreal dimension:

> – and all for nothing –
> For Hecuba?
> What's Hecuba to him, or he to her,
> That he should weep for her?

> (*HAM* 2.2.492–5)

Why do we cry, worry, rejoice, hate and hope for fictional characters? How is it possible to feel emotions for people who do

not even exist? Over the last fifty years, the philosophical debate
on the link between emotions and fiction seems to have revolved
around Hamlet's point of view. It is not accidental, then, that his
words are quoted in the opening of Colin Radford's 'How Can We
be Moved by the Fate of Anna Karenina?', which appeared in the
Proceedings of the Aristotelian Society in 1975 and officially initiated
the debate on the so-called 'paradox of fiction'. Radford starts from
the assumption that there are significant differences between the
emotions we feel in response to (what we believe are) real events
and those we experience in response to events that we know to be
imaginary. For the sake of simplicity, we may call the former 'real-
life emotions' and the latter 'emotions towards fictional entities'.
Real-life emotions are usually (though not always) more intense and
longer in duration. In addition, there are major differences at the
behavioural level, as emotions towards fictional entities tend to lack
the motivational drive triggered by real-life emotions. Although
emotions towards fictional entities produce some distinctive and
often visible bodily symptoms and expressions, we typically do
not act upon them as we would do with real-life emotions (e.g. we
would not cry for help nor step onto the theatre stage to prevent
Mercutio from being killed, however frightening and upsetting the
performance may be). According to Radford, however, the most
striking difference is that real-life emotions presuppose a belief
in the existence of their object, while emotions towards fictional
entities do not:

> it is what is common to being moved in either situation which
> makes problematic one of the differences, viz., the fact that belief
> is not necessary in the fictional situation. (Radford 1975: 75–6)

Let us consider the three following propositions as they are usually
phrased in the literature (e.g. Carroll 1990; Currie 1990; Levinson 1997;

Cova and Teroni 2016; Friend 2016; Konrad, Petraschka and Werner 2018; Teroni 2019):

P1. We feel genuine emotions towards fictional entities.

P2. We know that fictional entities do not actually exist.

P3. Genuine emotions are grounded on our belief that their object actually exists.

If taken in isolation, these propositions seem reasonable (at least *prima facie*), but yield a contradiction when they are brought together, as it is obvious that they cannot be all true at the same time. This is what is normally referred to as the 'paradox of fiction'.

Since Radford's seminal paper (and Kendall Walton's 'Fearing Fictions', published in 1978), several attempts have been made either to solve the paradox by denying one of the propositions in the triad (and yet accounting for its initial plausibility) or to deny that there is a paradox in the first place by claiming that there are no reasons – not even *prima facie* – to endorse the thesis that emotions are causally or conceptually grounded on beliefs in the existence of their intentional objects. Derek Matravers, for example, has recently argued that nobody has ever endorsed a claim such as P3, not even in the golden days of cognitive theory: for this reason, Radford's arguments are flawed and the paradox is to be dismissed (Matravers 2014: 104–6; for similar attempts to solve the paradox see Stecker 2011 and Tullman and Buckwalter 2014). It is beyond doubt that, perhaps with the exception of proponents of a very narrow cognitivist approach (e.g. Nussbaum 2004; Solomon 2003), few emotion theorists would endorse P3, at least in the formulation provided above. However, although the idea that emotions always entail believing in the existence of their intentional object is untenable, it is hard to deny that, in ordinary real-life situations, emotions directed towards objects that we take to be real are likely to decrease in intensity or even to disappear if we learn that those objects do not really exist. Radford discusses the example of a man who tells us a harrowing story about his sister, making us feel a certain amount of discomfort. He later tells us that he has made up the whole story and does not even have a sister. Once we learn the truth, we no longer feel harrowed (and may in fact feel somewhat annoyed). What Radford finds incoherent is that we treat emotions towards fictional entities differently from emotions for entities which we know to be real, and experience the former despite knowing since the very beginning that their object does not exist. In this respect, Cova and Teroni (2016) have proved that P3 is supported by a good deal of experimental evidence coming from psychological research on emotion regulation and cognitive reappraisal strategies, which shows that when information concerning the ontological status of the object (i.e. whether it is real or fictional) is fed into one's appraisal system, this modifies the emotional response (e.g. Dandoy and Goldstein 1990; Vritčka, Sander and Vuilleumier 2011). Of course, the claim that in ordinary real-life contexts it is often the case that our emotions decrease in intensity or even disappear when we re-appraise their intentional object as false or unreal can be combined with both P1 and P2 without yielding any paradox. For this claim does not entail that we can never experience emotions in the absence of the relevant existential beliefs, nor that it is always the case that a change in our existential beliefs determines a change in our affective responses. And yet we would still need to explain what exactly goes on when we experience emotions towards fictional entities, and what is the difference between this scenario and that of real-life emotions.

Attempts to solve the paradox by denying one of the three propositions can be divided into three different theoretical frameworks, depending on which of the propositions they reject. The so-called 'illusion theories of fiction', based on Coleridge's notion of 'the willing suspension of disbelief' (Coleridge [1817] 2005: 145), appeal to notions such as those of 'half-belief', 'forgetfulness' or 'illusion', and reject P2. In doing so, however, they find themselves unable to explain behavioural disanalogies between real-life emotions and emotions towards fictional entities. Besides, the 'illusion' or 'forgetfulness' they postulate is patently at odds with the pleasure we derive from the emotional experience of fiction even when the emotion we feel is, for example, one of fear or pity (whose hedonic tone in real-life situations is usually not one of pleasure). The main objection against this approach is therefore that emotions towards fictional entities seem to presuppose that we know that we are dealing with fiction, in which case, however, P2 cannot be denied.

Pretend theorists, instead, try to solve the paradox by denying P1, and describe emotions towards fictional entities as quasi-emotions resulting from a make-believe engagement with the fictional product (Walton 1978, 1990). According to this view, we cannot give up the thesis that, when experiencing art, we are aware of it being fictional, since this awareness alone can account for behavioural disanalogies between real-life emotions and emotions towards fictional entities (Walton 1978: 8–10). Nor can we reject the common-sense assumption that genuine emotions presuppose a belief in the existence of their particular objects and their relation to some evaluative property: for example, in order for fear to be genuine, we need to believe that its object exists and is dangerous (Walton 1978: 6–7; 1990: 245). Thus, the only way out of the contradiction available to pretend theorists consists in defining our emotions towards fictional entities as themselves fictional and based on pretend beliefs that we derive from our engagement in a make-believe game with the product of fiction. For this reason, pretend theorists do not deny P3, but rather qualify the beliefs it involves as make-beliefs regarding the assertion of fictional propositions: emotions towards fictional entities are generated by the pretence of asserting (seriously) that something is the case, that is, by a pretended commitment to the truth of a fictional statement (Walton 1978: 19). The main objection to this approach is that it is not phenomenologically accurate, as the idea of pretence and simulation cannot account for our perception that our emotions towards fictional entities feel genuine (e.g. Carroll 1990).[2]

A third attempt to solve the paradox consists in accepting both P1 and P2 while qualifying the beliefs involved by P3 as prefaced by a fiction operator. The idea is to characterize emotions by distinguishing them not by virtue of the psychological attitude they imply (which would be that of a serious, non-simulated belief), but on the basis of the (fictional) properties of the content of this attitude. This strategy is adopted, for example, by Matravers (1991), who describes emotions towards fictional entities as based on the belief of what is fictionally the case – that is, a belief that is devoid of ontological commitments. In Matravers' view, the difference between real-life emotions and emotions towards fictional entities lies in the fact that it is impossible to causally interact with imaginary events. What emotions towards fictional entities lack, then, is not the disposition to action, but rather instrumental beliefs (i.e. 'beliefs about how something that is in our power to do would satisfy our desire', Matravers 1991: 28). Since instrumental beliefs as such are not components of our emotions, Matravers concludes that

> when our emotions are aroused by a description of a situation rather than by the situation itself, they are typically not accompanied by any relevant instrumental beliefs. Fiction is just a special case of this, where our emotions are never accompanied by the relevant instrumental beliefs. (Matravers 1991: 29)[3]

The view that contents and not beliefs are fictional is endorsed also by Alex Neill (1993). In accordance with Matravers' distinction between disposition to act and instrumental beliefs, Neill argues that, given the ontological gap between the actual and the fictional world, we cannot desire what is logically impossible (e.g. we cannot desire to help a fictional character), but we can indeed leave room for the desire that, *fictionally*, things could go in a different way (Neill 1993: 7–11). This kind of desire is based on the belief that something is fictionally the case, and does not concern its (real) representation, but only its fictional content: desiring that things should go differently for Anna Karenina is not the same as desiring that Tolstoy's novel had a different plot structure. Neill argues that we may take different attitudes towards works of art: we can consider them objectively, as more or less artistically valuable artefacts, but we can also experience them emotionally, so as to become immersed in them. This distinction is interesting because it allows us to focus on an aspect of aesthetic experience that is often referred to through the metaphor of being 'caught up' in the work of art, which would 'transport' us into its own world (e.g. Neill 1988; Ryan 1991; Gerrig 1993; Green and Brock 2002). The experiential authenticity of emotions depends directly on the phenomenon of 'immersion' in an imaginary world – a phenomenon that any tenable theory must be able to account for. Neill's implicit endorsement of Matravers argument of the fictional operator presupposes a constant and explicit form of awareness of the ontological status of the imaginary product (i.e. believing that, *in the fiction,* things are as they are), which is strikingly at odds with the intensity and immediacy of the aesthetic 'rapture'.

While these cursory remarks on the debate on emotions towards fictional entities do not aim to offer an exhaustive reconstruction of the theoretical solutions that have been proposed in this regard (for a complete and up-to-date discussion see Friend 2016 and Teroni 2019), they provide an excellent test bed for measuring the explanatory reliability of some of the main contemporary takes on emotions. In particular, the problem of the paradox of fiction allows us to assess the adequacy of two main orientations: on the one hand, prescriptive approaches to the phenomenon of emotions; on the other hand, representationalist views that insist on equating emotions with beliefs.

Two approaches to the search for a definition of 'emotion' can be pursued: a descriptive one and a prescriptive one. The former aims to achieve an accurate understanding of the way 'emotion' is used in ordinary language and how it is conceptualized by common-sense psychology. The latter aims to turn common-sense categories into epistemically useful tools by picking out a set of features that can be analysed, explained and eventually generalized (Widen and Russell 2010; Scarantino 2012; see above, pp. 2–10). These are two different projects and should not be confused, and yet it is quite obvious that the way in which the paradox of fiction is phrased leads us to overlook this distinction. In the literature, P1 and P3 are typically formulated using the qualifier 'genuine' to distinguish emotions 'proper' from phenomena which do not qualify as such, and this approach, in turn, is underpinned by the implicit assumption that a prescriptive definition can at the same time provide us with descriptive understanding. Unsurprisingly, all the different ways out of the paradox that have been proposed rest on the same essentialist assumption: by defining a set of necessary and sufficient properties as a condition for membership in a given category, one can either (i) stipulate that what does not fit one's definition is not to be considered as a member or (ii) neglect one or more features of the phenomenon under study in order to make it fit the category as this is theoretically construed. Thus, in line with the first variant of this strategy and with the aim of safeguarding the role that beliefs play in emotional experience according to the stipulated definition, Walton denies that emotions towards fictional entities are real emotions and downgrades them to quasi-emotions. For pretty much the same reason, illusion theories fail to account for the behavioural differences between real-life emotions and emotions towards fictional entities, as well as to explain variations in the hedonic tone of the same emotion in the transition between reality and fiction. Similarly, the theories that introduce the fictional operator are bound to give up any phenomenological analysis of the experience of aesthetic 'rapture'. In sum, the very problem connected with emotions towards fictional entities depends at least in part on adopting a prescriptive perspective that stipulates the existence of a class of emotions proper with respect to which emotions towards fictional entities would represent an anomaly.

The main theories that animate the debate on the paradox of fiction are all grounded on the same assumption, in that they seek to get around the problem of the non-existence of fictional entities. They do so because they assume that imagination and doxastic processes are substantially homogeneous: 'imagining (that) p' essentially means 'believing (that) p'. Consequently, unless we suspend our disbelief regarding the existence of p or believe that it is fictionally the case that p, what we feel are quasi-emotions, not genuine ones. What we need to focus on is therefore p, that is, the content to which emotions are directed, along with epistemic beliefs concerning its ontological status. It is the ontological gap between the content of real-life emotions and emotions towards fictional entities that renders their phenomenological similarity problematic, and this is a shortcoming that a representationalist approach to imagination can hardly avoid. We can, however, embrace a different perspective if we shift our focus from imagination as a belief-like representational attitude to imagination as a form of perceptual re-enactment.

The analogies between perception and imagination have been highlighted by several phenomenological and neuroscientific studies.

Among the former, the most famous experiment is undoubtedly that of American psychologist Mary Cheves West Perky (Perky 1910). Perky asked the subjects in the study to focus on a specific point on a frosted glass screen and to imagine a series of objects (a tomato, a book, a banana, an orange, a leaf and a lemon). Unbeknown to the subjects, Perky and her colleagues projected onto the screen some barely visible coloured images corresponding to the objects that the participants were trying to imagine. None of the participants realized what was going on behind the scenes. Some reported with some surprise that they had imagined an elm leaf although they intended to imagine a maple leaf; and all reported with surprise that although they had expected to imagine a banana in a horizontal position, they had in fact imagined it lying vertically. None of them, however, realized that they had perceived the objects, rather than imagining them. According to the traditional interpretation of the so-called 'Perky effect', if perceptual and imaginative activity can be so easily confused, then they must be very similar in terms of subjective experience (but see Segal 1971, 1972 and Hopkins 2012). The thesis of the similarity between perception and imagination is backed by substantial neuroscientific evidence: the brain areas involved in perception are in fact largely involved in imagination as well (e.g. Kosslyn, Ganis and Thompson 2001 and Kosslyn, Thompson and Ganis 2006), and cortex activation patterns are also similar (e.g. Page et al. 2011). To be sure, this similarity does not only concern sight and visualization, but also extends to other forms of perception (hearing, smell, taste and touch) and sensory imagination (i.e. perceptual experience in the absence of corresponding stimuli, as when we imagine or remember things).

If we assume the analogy between perception and imagination, the way we interpret the former will inevitably affect our understanding of the latter. Consider, for instance, pictorialism. Pictorialism, whose main exponent is Stephen Kosslyn, has gained much currency among representationalist theories of perception and imagination. One of the reasons for its success is that it fits nicely with our intuitions about the way in which we perceive the world. The fundamental idea that sight, understood as the paradigmatic instance of perception, works with quasi-photographic mechanisms, is perfectly in tune with our intuitions: our eyes are windows opened to the external world, through which we see the world-as-it-is, whereas mental representations are in many respect similar to images (Kosslyn 1980, 1994, 2005). Such an account matches perfectly with the so-called 'jigsaw model' of imagination (Jajdelska et al. 2010): just as visual perception consists in building up internal representations based on the information we retrieve from the external environment, imagination involves creating mental images based on representations stored in the memory and variously combined with each other (e.g. by following the 'instructions' of the novel we are reading, or freely if we are just daydreaming). The problem with pictorialism is that its basic assumptions are incompatible with what we know about the anatomy of the eye, as well as with the results that emerge from various studies in experimental psychology. As regards the structure of the human eye, for instance, we know that the cones and rods are not uniformly distributed over the retina, and that only in its middle area does visual acuity reach its maximum, because of the greater density of cones in the fovea. The fact that the entire visual field appears homogeneous and sharp is due to the saccadic movements, thanks to which the fovea focuses on the relevant targets. From an evolutionary perspective, this can be explained by the need to monitor the external environment as a whole, while focusing only on potentially relevant stimuli; a 'photographic' representation of the world would have no particular adaptive value. That this is the case is also suggested by research on the phenomenon of inattentional blindness and sensory adaptation. The amusing experiment of the invisible gorilla, devised and conducted by Christopher Chabris and Daniel Simons, reveals for example that, even if we do not realize it, our perceptual attention is selective and depends on the interests and goals we are pursuing (Simons and Chabris 1999). While watching a video in which six players, three in white and three in black jerseys, pass the ball to each other, the subjects involved in the experiment were asked to count the number of passes made by the white team. Approximately half of the participants failed to realize that, at a certain point, a man dressed as a gorilla appears on the scene, stops in front of the camera, beats his chest and leaves. It is therefore possible, and indeed quite common, that when we are focusing on a given activity we end up ignoring other elements and features of the environment (even remarkable and surprising ones, as in the case of the gorilla), insofar as they are not relevant to the performance of our task. From an adaptive point of view, not only does the accurate representation of the external world seem unnecessary: phenomena such as sensory adaptation (i.e. the reduction of sensitivity to a stimulus to which we are exposed over long periods of time) suggest that it might even turn out to be detrimental:

> Adaptation means that there is a progressive shift in neural activity away from accurate portrayal of maintained physical events. Thus the nervous system may fail to register neural activity even though the stimulus continues. Such a striking discrepancy is no accident; sensory systems emphasize change in stimuli because changes are more likely to be significant for survival. Sensory adaptation is a form of information suppression that prevents the nervous system from becoming overwhelmed by stimuli that offer very little 'news' about the world. (Rosenzweig, Breedlove and Watson 2005: 225)

An alternative and particularly promising interpretation of the mechanisms of perception and imagination is offered by enactivist theories. From this viewpoint, both perception and imagination are a matter of embodied exploration of the world rather than of its representation. We already mentioned that action is key to perception, since the latter does not consist in the passive registration of information and data coming from outside, but is itself an activity of the organism, whose sensitivity to specific environmental features depends on its biological and morphological characteristics and on potential sensorimotor interactions with the external world (e.g. Noë 2004). Contrary to the view according to which imagining simply means seeing objects with the mind's eye, imagination is considered as an activity, and in this sense put on par with perception. But if imagination consists in the sensorimotor exploration of the imagined world, and if this exploration depends on the same kind of resources that make sensory perception possible, then arguably the structure of these experiences must be strikingly similar. The enactivist interpretation of perception and imagination paints an accurate phenomenological picture: by stressing the direct and immediate character of both processes, it explains the involvement of bodily feelings and affective states, as well as their intensity, in a way that is much more credible than what pictorialism and the 'jigsaw model' of imagination can achieve (as shown, for example, by the results that this approach yields when applied to narrative theory: see Caracciolo 2013, 2014; Kuzmičová 2014; Kukkonen 2014 and Troscianko 2014a, b). The idea that images are received from the outside (or constructed by combining existing representations) and then mentally inspected falls short of what we need to fully account for the feeling of 'vividness' that typically characterizes the experience of imagination. If, instead, we interpret imagination as a perceptual re-enactment (again, as opposed to the simple observation of a mental image), it becomes possible to shed light on its sensory dimension, which in turn leads to the feeling of 'involvement' that lays the basis for emotions towards fictional entities: for insofar as imaginative feelings (and emotions) are grounded on the analogy between imagination and perception as structurally similar activities, then the content of imagination tends to become irrelevant. But if this is the case, then from an enactivist perspective the problem of the ontological status of fictional entities is no longer intractable, as the process at stake would no longer entail the formulation of epistemic beliefs, but would rather be a matter of perceiving the imagined world, enacting it through actions, and experiencing it through senses. And it is precisely by virtue of the sensory dimension of the imaginative simulation of perceptual experience that we can feel emotions towards fictional entities and accept them as an integral part of our affective life.

Further readings

Defining emotions

The problem of defining emotion is presented and explored from different disciplinary perspectives in two dedicated sections of *Emotion Review*. See 'Special Section. On Defining Emotion', in *Emotion Review* 2.4 (2010: 363–85) and 'Special section. On Defining Emotion', in *Emotion Review* 4.4 (2012: 337–93).

For a discussion of whether emotions should be considered natural kinds see Griffiths (1997), Russell (2003), Prinz (2004a: Chapter 3), Barrett (2006) and Scarantino (2012).

On emotion, language and metaphor, see Lakoff and Kövecses (1987), Kövecses (2000) and Lakoff (2016).

Darwin

Darwin's complete works, including manuscripts, letters and private notes, are freely available online at http://darwin-online.org.uk (van Wyhe 2002).

Paul Ekman's edition of *The Expression of the Emotions in Man and Animals* (Ekman 1998) features the commentaries of the editor, who takes the opportunity to present his theses and discuss how they fit with Darwin's own views.

A comprehensive presentation of *The Expression of the Emotions in Man and Animals* and of the relation between research on emotions and theory of evolution from Darwin's perspective is offered by Browne (1985).

For an overview of Darwin's views on mind, morals, and emotions, from *On the Origin of Species* up to *The Expression of the Emotions in Man and Animals*, see Richards (2009).

For a survey of the philosophical, psychological and scientific sources that most influenced Darwin's views on the expression of emotions, and for an analysis of how the formulation of the three principles laid out in *Expression* was influenced by Darwin's anti-theological perspective, see Dixon (2003: 159–79).

Drawing on an investigation into the way the scientific culture of the second half of the nineteenth century transformed the moral notion of *sympathy*, Boddice (2016: 26–52) proposes an interesting analysis of Darwin's views on the evolution of species and of civilization, as well as on the relation between *The Expression of the Emotions in Man and Animals* and *The Descent of Man*.

Gross (2010) emphasizes that in Darwin's view interpretation and imagination play an important role in the recognition of the bodily manifestations of emotions.

Evolutionism

For an overview of Cosmides and Tooby's evolutionary approach to the phenomenon of emotions, see Tooby and Cosmides (2008).

Sznycer et al. (2017b) outline the advantages of analysing emotions on the basis of their adaptive function, advocate a universalist perspective and discuss the similarities and differences between evolutionary theory, constructionism and dimensional theories of appraisal.

For some examples of how the evolutionary approach applies to the analysis of the nature and properties of specific emotions, see

Sznycer et al. (2017c; compassion, envy and self-interest); Sznycer et al. (2017a; pride); Sell, Cosmides, and Tooby (2014; anger).

Universalism

Ekman's neurocultural theory is laid out in Ekman (1971). Ekman's views on the universality of facial expressions are discussed in greater detail in Ekman (1980) and Ekman (2003).

Russell (1994) offers a critique of the thesis of the universality of facial expressions, providing convincing arguments both on the theoretical level and regarding the experimental design of the main studies concerning the cross-cultural uniformity of emotion recognition. Ekman's retort (1994) is followed by Russell's own reply (1995).

Emotion Review issued a special section devoted to the topic of facial expressions: 'Special Section. Facial expressions', in *Emotion Review* 5.1 (2013: 3–103).

Basic Emotion Theory

For a recent presentation of Paul Ekman's theory of basic emotions, see Ekman and Cordaro (2011).

For a presentation of Izard's differential theory see Izard (1977: 43–66); a more recent discussion can be found in Izard (2007).

The special section 'Honoring Carroll Izard's Contributions to the Field of Emotions' in *Emotion Review* 7.2 (2015: 101–42) is devoted to Carroll Izard's work.

The standard reference text for Panksepp's theory is Panksepp (1998). For a more streamlined presentation see Panksepp and Watt (2011).

Ekman and Cordaro (2011) and Panksepp and Watt (2011) appear, with many other contributions, in the special section of *Emotion Review* devoted to Basic Emotion Theory: 'Special Section. Basic Emotion Theory', in *Emotion Review* 2.4 (2011: 363–454).

Constructionism

For a presentation of Russell's approach see Russell (2003).

For a recent presentation of Barrett's theory see Barrett (2017a, b)

A comprehensive introduction to psychological constructionism and its variants is offered by Barrett and Russell (2015).

Emotion Review has devoted three special sections to constructionism: 'Special Section. Social-Constructivist Approaches to Emotion', in *Emotion Review* 4.3 (2012: 215–306), 'Special Section. Psychological Constructivism', in *Emotion Review* 5.4 (2013: 333–89) and 'Special Section. Four Perspectives on the Psychology of Emotion', in *Emotion Review* 6.4 (2014: 291–331).

Cognition-arousal theory

For a recent discussion of Schachter and Singer's theory, see the special section 'Cognition-Arousal Theory', in *Emotion Review* 9.1 (2017: 3–63).

James

For two radically different views on William James's theory of emotions, see Ellsworth (1994) and Reisenzein, Meyer, and Schützwohl (1995).

Ratcliffe (2005) proposes an interesting interpretation of James's theory of emotions, focusing on James's acknowledgement of the cognitive dimension of bodily processes.

Livingston (2019) reads Lange's work in the original Danish version and stresses that the differences between Lange's theory and James's are actually more significant than the similarities that are traditionally emphasized.

Emotion Review has devoted a special section to 'William James and His Legacy', in *Emotion Review* 6.1 (2014: 3–52).

Emotions and formal objects

For the introduction of the concept of 'formal objects' into the debate on emotions see Kenny (1963).

For a discussion of formal objects as conditions for the intelligibility and correctness of emotions, see de Sousa (1987: Chapter 5).

Teroni (2007) offers a detailed analysis of the role of axiological properties *qua* formal objects of emotions.

Appraisal theories

For an overview of the historical development of appraisal theories and an account of the main ideas on which these are based, see Scherer, Schorr and Johnstone (2001).

An overview of the various theoretical approaches within the appraisal tradition can be found in Moors (2014).

Emotion Review has devoted a special section to appraisal theories: 'Special Section. Appraisal', in *Emotion Review* 5.2 (2013: 119–91).

With his paper 'Feeling and Thinking: Preferences Need no Inferences', published in 1980 in *American Psychologist*, Robert Zajonc started with Richard Lazarus a debate known as the cognition–emotion debate (Zajonc 1984; Lazarus 1982, 1984). Zajonc maintains that affective and cognitive processes constitute independent systems and that the former can precede the latter, that is they can arise without any prior cognitive activity (where by 'cognition' Zajonc refers only to higher-order cognitive processes). For a summary of the debate see Lazarus (1999); for a critical reconstruction see Prinz (2004a: 33–41).

For a critique of the mind-body dualism implicitly endorsed by the appraisal tradition, see Colombetti (2014: Chapter 4).

Theories of emotions as value judgements

For a discussion of Solomon's and Nussbaum's theories and, more generally, of the identification of emotions with value judgements, see Roberts (2003: 83–106).

Within the framework of evaluative theory, some approaches consider value judgements as essential yet non-exclusive components of emotion, and include other aspects (e.g. physiological or desire-related features) in the analysis of affective phenomena: for example, Lyons 1980.

Theories of emotions as perceptions of value

Philosophy and Phenomenological Research has devoted a section to the discussion of *Gut Reactions* by Jesse Prinz (2004a). The section includes a précis of *Gut Reactions*, two critical contributions (by

Justin D'Arms and David Hills) and Prinz's reply: *Philosophy and Phenomenological Research* (2008: 707–32).

Deonna (2006) views favourably the analogy between emotion and perception. Salmela (2011) suggests instead a more critical reading.

For an illustration of the Müller-Lyer illusion and of the duck–rabbit ambiguous figure, see, respectively, Donaldson and Macpherson (2017) and Donaldson (2016).

Dewey

Dewey's work is freely available online at http://www.nlx.com/collections/133 (Hickman 1996).

For a detailed account of Dewey's theory of emotions see Franks (1991), Cunningham (1995), and Garrison (2003).

The attitudinal theory of emotions

For the distinction between content and attitude (or mode) in philosophy of mind, see Searle (1983) and Crane (2009).

Rossi and Tappolet (2018) criticize Deonna and Teroni's theory and examine it in relation to the theory of emotions as perceptions of values.

The motivational theory of emotions

Scarantino (2015) interprets emotions as action control systems with control precedence in the light of an evolutionary approach and proposes 'the new BET', a basic emotion theory which, in his view, can withstand constructionist challenges.

The enactivist revolution

Phenomenology and the Cognitive Sciences has devoted a special section (edited by Richard Menary) to 4E Cognition: *Phenomenology and the Cognitive Sciences* 9.4 (2010: 459–671).

A good starting point for addressing the question of the ontological status of emotional affordances is Hufendiek (2017).

For the study of emotion in the framework of dynamical systems theory, see Colombetti (2009) and (2014: Chapter 3).

As regards the potential of material objects, artefacts and cultural and social institutions to shape affective states, see, among others, Griffiths and Scarantino (2009), Krueger (2014), Colombetti and Krueger (2015), Colombetti and Roberts (2015) and Krueger and Szanto (2016).

Notes

Introduction

1 Cf. *Dictionnaire historique de la langue française s.v.* 'émotion'.

2 Cf. the 1843 edition of the *Diccionario de la lengua castellana por la Real Academia Española s.v.* 'emoción'.

3 Cf. Dardi (1992: 525–6).

4 A notable exception was David Hume, who already used the term in a sense similar to the current one in his *Treatise of Human Nature* (1739–40).

5 Cf. Dixon 2003.

6 Jesse Prinz has called this 'the Problem of Parts'. Cf. Prinz (2004a: Chapter 1) for a discussion of how different emotion theories offer different responses to this problem.

7 The distinction between feeling tradition, evaluative tradition, and motivational tradition is discussed by Scarantino (2016).

8 Armstrong, Gleitman and Gleitman (1983), for example, show that prototype effects occur even when it comes to categories such as EVEN NUMBER, ODD NUMBER, FEMALE or GEOMETRICAL FLAT FIGURE, which are normally categorized by means of classical definitions (i.e. based on the identification of necessary and sufficient properties that characterize each member of the category).

9 Eric Margolis and Stephen Laurence present the so-called prototype theory, highlighting both its merits and its potentially problematic aspects, in the introductory chapter, entitled 'Concepts and Cognitive Science', of *Concepts: Core Readings*, of which they are editors (Margolis and Laurence 1999).

10 The natural kinds with which we are most familiar are probably those of chemistry. For example, in chemistry water is identified as a compound

with the molecular formula H_2O; a substance is water if and only if it has this molecular structure; what we know about water (e.g. boiling point, surface cohesion force between molecules, viscosity coefficient at different temperatures and so on) is generalizable and can be extended to all substances that qualify as 'water'. For an essentialist definition of natural kinds see Kripke (1980); for a more liberal definition, based on the notion of clusters of homeostatic properties, see Boyd (1989).

11 Ekman (1992). Ekman later extended the list of basic emotions to include up to fifteen candidates (e.g. Ekman 1999: 55).

12 Consider for instance the strategy adopted by Griffiths (1997), who criticizes the idea that the category of EMOTION is a natural kind on the basis of the distinction between 'affect programs' and 'higher cognitive emotions' ('complex emotions' in Griffiths 2004). But see Clark (2010).

13 'Emotion researchers face a scandal: We have no agreed upon definition for the term – emotion – that defines our field. We therefore do not know what events count as examples of emotion and what events theories of emotion must explain' (Russell 2012: 337).

14 Cairns (2019: 2–5) makes this point and discusses its implications for the historical and cross-cultural study of emotion.

15 Of course, albeit based on the modes of our physical interaction with the environment, the elaboration of conceptual metaphors is culturally specific.

Expression

1 Marchant (1916: 182).

2 Bell (1806). A second edition appeared in 1824 under the title *Essays on the Anatomy and Philosophy of Expression*.

3 The idea that there is an immediate and constitutive connection between states of mind and their bodily manifestations, as specifically provided for by divine design in order to allow human beings to express their emotions, is followed on Bell's account by the thesis that human emotions are universal; by contrast, the expressions that in animals purportedly show emotional states are in fact nothing more than physical manifestations of their needs: 'I shall venture to affirm . . . that a remarkable difference is to be found between the anatomy and range of expression in man and in

animals: That in the former, there seems to be a systematic provision for that mode of communication and that natural language, which is to be read in the changes of countenance; that there is no emotion in the mind of man which has not its appropriate signs; and that there are even muscles in the human face, to which no other use can be assigned, than to serve as the organs of this language: That on the other hand there is in the lower animals no range of expression which is not fairly referable as a mere accessory to the voluntary or needful actions of the animal; . . . It is, in short, of man alone that we can with strict propriety say, the countenance is an index of the mind, having expression corresponding with each emotion of the soul' (Bell 1806: 85–8).

4 For an analysis of Darwin's criticism of Bell's views and some of the paradoxes that arise, see Dixon (2003: 172–5).

5 However, unlike many contemporary experimental psychologists and universalist theorists, Darwin appreciates the dynamic interplay between biological universalism and the sociocultural dimension and assesses it in a highly sophisticated manner: in addition to stressing the variability of the rules of performance, he is aware that the ability to recognize complex emotions depends not only on the observation of their manifestations, but also, and to an important extent, on contextual and pragmatic information. See for instance Darwin ([1872]2009): 'It is doubtful whether the greater number of the above complex states of mind [i.e. jealously, envy, avarice, revenge, suspicion, deceit, slyness, guilt, vanity, conceit, ambition, pride, humility] are revealed by any fixed expression, sufficiently distinct to be described or delineated. When Shakespeare speaks of Envy as lean-faced, or black, or pale, and Jealousy as "the green-eyed monster"; and when Spenser describes suspicion as "foul ill-favoured, and grim", they must have felt this difficulty. Nevertheless, the above feelings – at least many of them – can be detected by the eye; for instance, conceit; *but we are often guided in a much greater degree than we suppose by our previous knowledge of the persons or circumstances*' (260; emphasis added).

6 From Darwin's standpoint, the universalist thesis coexists with the idea that different human groups reflect different stages of moral and intellectual development. This emerges explicitly in *The Descent of Man*, where Darwin discusses the relation between evolutionary history and human history (see Gross 2010 and Boddice 2016).

7 For example, love is almost always accompanied by the intense desire to touch the beloved person, but different social groups employ different strategies for seeking physical contact: in Europe, Darwin observes, we are used to kissing, while this is an unknown practice in other parts of the

world. In New Zealand and Lapland, for example, it is common practice to press one's nose against the nose of the beloved person, or to touch each other's hands, chest, or belly (Darwin [1872]2009: 213–4).

8   See also Darwin's note on James Mackintosh's *Dissertation on the Progress of Ethical Philosophy* (1836): 'Emotions, having been formed by actions, will always lead to them' (Di Gregorio 1990: 558–9).

9   Already at the time of *Notebook N*, Darwin had understood that emotions are constituted by their own manifestations: '[Emotions are the heredetary [*sic*] effects on the mind accompanying certain bodily actions]. . . . "without 'slight' flush, acceleration of pulse. or rigidity of muscles. – man cannot be said to be angry – He may have pain or pleasure these are sensations [not emotions]"' (Barrett et al. 2008: 581–2).

10 In *The Emotions and the Will*, published in 1859 (as was *On the Origin of Species*), Alexander Bain had already stressed the importance of the dynamic interaction between emotion understood as a subjective state and its bodily manifestations: 'These changes in the allocation of the members that receive the recoil of a state of mental exhilaration have no slight influence in changing the character of the consciousness; for it is not the original stimulus alone, but this, in conjunction with all the reflected waves, that determines the nature of the resulting mental condition' (Bain 1859: 14–15).

11 The Environment of Evolutionary Adaptedness (EEA) is the environment in which a trait (in our case, an emotion) has been selected. It amounts to the statistical set of selective pressures that led to the production and stabilization of a given form of adaptation.

12 On Darwin's attempt to combine universalism with the recognition of the important role played by the context in the observer's interpretation of bodily manifestations of emotions, see above, p.169, note 5.

13 Ekman was a pupil of psychologist Silvan Tomkins, who was the first to introduce the notion of 'primary affects', claiming that these serve a motivational function and are related to specific sets of coordinated movements regulated by corresponding affective programmes rooted in our genetic heritage (Tomkins [1961–1991] 2008).

14 In this context, a well-known experiment showed that Japanese participants smile more than American participants when watching distressing videos if they are aware of being observed; on reviewing the slow-motion footage, experimenters realized that smiling inhibits an initially sad expression

(Ekman 1971). For a critique of Ekman's interpretation of the results of this experiment and, in general, of the dichotomy between biologically inherited and universal facial expressions and expressions that are culturally conditioned by display rules, see Crivelli, Fridlund (2019).

15 In particular, the research of ethologist Irenäus Eibl-Eibesfeldt. According to Eibl-Eibesfeldt, the observation of similar expressive behaviour in children who have been blind from birth and therefore have no opportunity to learn by imitation supports the idea that this type of behaviour is innate (e.g. Eibl-Eibesfeldt 1973). More recently, a study of the spontaneous facial expressions of individuals blind from birth was carried out by David Matsumoto (Matsumoto and Willingham 2009).

16 See e.g. Thayer (1980) and Russell (1991). For a more recent account, see Liu et al. (2019).

17 These would be constant at a general level, but not in their specific variants: for example, the loss of an important person in one's life universally elicits sorrow; however, the question of who specifically is important to us and why will depend on a number of personal and cultural factors.

18 In this respect, Ekman mentions prototype theory and points out that the categories of basic emotions do not correspond to the radial categories investigated by Rosch (Ekman 1992: 173).

19 The same emotions (with the exception of surprise) featured in the animated film *Inside Out*, to which Ekman contributed as a scientific consultant.

20 Panksepp relies on the 'triune brain' model originally formulated by Paul D. MacLean (cf. MacLean 1990).

21 By using small caps, Panksepp wishes to point out that it is not common-sense notions that are at stake, but rather interspecific neurochemical processes in charge of modulating functional behaviour such as reproduction, escape from danger, and so on (Panksepp 1998: 27–8, 79–80).

Alternatives and criticism

1 Recently, however, Paul Ekman has admitted that affect programmes are conditioned by environmental inputs and may therefore change in the course of an individual's life (e.g. Ekman and Cordaro 2011).

2 For example, see Murphy, Nimmo-Smith and Lawrence (2003) and Larsen et al. (2008). Panksepp (2007) presents and discusses several studies left out by Barrett's review, which substantiate the claim that there is a correspondence between certain patterns of neurophysiological and neurochemical activation and specific behavioural and emotional states.

3 Importantly, Barrett's approach differs from Schachter and Singer's in several ways. See Lindquist and Barrett (2008) for discussion.

4 The question of the existence of specific physiological alterations for each emotion has sparked a lively debate since the publication of William James's 'What is an Emotion?' in 1884. Indeed, one of the most famous criticisms levelled against James's theory come from physiologist Walter Cannon, who pointed out that many of the bodily symptoms typical of a given emotion often occur also in other circumstances, which are not emotional in nature: for example, one can shiver with cold as well as with fear; one can feel nausea because of disgust, but also because of food poisoning. For this reason, according to Cannon, there are no specific bodily reactions that allow us to diagnose specific sets of emotions.

5 For this and other criticisms, see Plutchik and Ax (1967).

6 See also MacCormack and Lindquist (2017).

Debate I

1 'Theory of mind' (sometimes termed 'mentalizing' or 'mindreading') refers to the ability to attribute mental states to oneself and to others, and, on this basis, to interpret and predict the behaviour of others.

2 The expression 'theory theory' was first introduced by Adam Morton (1980) to refer to the set of theories that explain the ability to interpret and predict the behaviour of others using the notions of moods, dispositions, character traits, relations between intentions and actions, and so on, that are typical of common-sense psychology.

3 Cf. Meltzoff 2007.

4 But cf. Meltzoff's argument that social cognition is built on the perception that others are 'like me' (Meltzoff 2007). Gopnik and Meltzoff's theory theory proposal entails the claim that innate mappings and the self-other equivalence are necessary mechanisms for development.

5 For example: 'One of the most important powers of the human mind is to conceive of and think about itself and other minds. Because the mental states of others (and indeed of ourselves) are completely hidden from the senses, they can only ever be inferred' (Leslie 1987: 139).

6 Narrative competencies, as they develop around the age of two, complement direct perception, allowing a more nuanced understanding of others and their situated reasons, attitudes and behaviour. For a formulation of the Narrative Practice Hypothesis see Hutto (2007) and Gallagher and Hutto (2007).

7 The German original reads as follows: 'Daß aber "Erlebnisse" da sind, das ist uns in den Ausdrucksphänomenen – wiederum nicht durch Schluß, sondern "unmittelbar"– gegeben im Sinne originären "Wahrnehmens": wir nehmen die Scham im Erröten wahr, im Lachen die Freude.'

8 See the contributions collected in Decety and Ickes (2009), Decety (2011), and Coplan and Goldie (2011) for discussion and criticism.

9 The French original reads as follows: 'En me promenant là autour, je rencontrai un vieillard fort vénérable qui regardait ce fameux combat avec autant de curiosité que moi. Il me fit signe de m'approcher: j'obéis, et nous nous assumes l'un auprès de l'autre. J'avais dessein de lui demander le motif qui l'avait amené en cette contrée, mais il me ferma la bouche par ces paroles: "Eh bien, vous le saurez, le motif qui m'amène en cette contrée!". Et là-dessus, il me raconta fort au long toutes les particularités de mon voyage. Je vous laisse à penser si je demeurai interdit. Cependant, pour accroître ma consternation, comme déjà je brûlais de lui demander quel démon lui révélait mes pensées: "Non, non, s'écria-t-il, ce n'est point un démon qui me révèle vos pensées". Ce nouveau tour de devin me le fit observer avec plus d'attention qu'auparavant, et je remarquai qu'il contrefaisait mon port, mes gestes, ma mine, situait tous ses membres, et figurait toutes les parties de son visage sur le patron des miennes; enfin, mon ombre en relief ne m'eût pas mieux représenté. "Je vois, continua-t-il, que vous êtes en peine de savoir pourquoi je vous contrefais, et je veux bien vous l'apprendre. Sachez donc qu'afin de connaître votre intérieur, j'arrange toutes les parties de mon corps dans un ordre semblable au vôtre; car, étant de toutes parts situé comme vous, j'excite en moi, par cette disposition de matière, la même pensée que produit en vous cette même disposition de matière"'.

10 Another reference to Campanella appears in *Les états et empires de la lune* and comes from Socrates' daimonion: 'I knew Campanella also; it was I that advised him, whilst he was in the Inquisition at Rome, to put his

Face and Body into the usual Postures of those, whose inside he needed to know, that by the same frame of Body, he might excite in himself, the thoughts which the same situation had raised in his Adversaries; because by so doing, he might better manage their Soul, when he came to know it; and at my desire he began a Book, which we Entituled, *De Sensu Rerum*.' ('Je connus aussi Campanelle; ce fut moi qui lui conseillai, pendant qu'il était à l'Inquistion dans Rome, de styler son visage et son corps aux postures ordinaires de ceux dont il avait besoin de connaître l'intérieur, afin d'exciter chez soi par une même assiette les pensées que cette même situation avait appelées dans ses adversaires, parce qu'ainsi il ménagerait mieux leur arme, quand il la connaîtrait, et il commnça, à ma pière, un Livre, que nous intitulâmes *de Sensu rerum*'; [1657-1662] 1886: 52). In his *De sensu rerum et magia*, Campanella attributes the special ability to know others through mimicry to a Telesian thinker named Jacopo di Gaeta: 'Acutus Caieta noster laudabat alteram physionomizandi rationem, ut si quando video hominem, statim imaginor me habere nasum, ut ille habet, et pilum et vultum et frontem et locutionem; et tunc qui affectus, et cogitationes in hac cogitatione mihi obrepunt, iudico esse proprios illi, quem ita imaginando contueor; et quidem non absque ratione, et experientia; spiritus enim format corpus, et iuxta affectus innatos ipsum fingit exprimitque' (Campanella 1637: 112). As regards the impact of voluntary movements on the subjective phenomenology of emotions, even William James mentions Campanella's mimetic technique and refers to the following passage from Burke, quoted by Dugald Stewart in *Elements of the Philosophy of the Human Mind*: 'This man, it seems, had not only made very accurate observations on human faces, but was very expert in mimicking such as were in any way remarkable. When he had a mind to penetrate into the inclinations of those lie had to deal with, he composed his face, his gesture, and his whole body, as nearly as he could, into the exact similitude of the person he intended to examine; and then carefully observed what turn of mind he seemed to acquire by the change. So that [. . .] he was able to enter into the dispositions and thoughts of people as effectually as if he had been changed into the very men. I have often observed [. . .] that, on mimicking the looks and gestures of angry, or placid, or frightened, or daring men, I have involuntarily found my mind turned to that passion whose appearance I strove to imitate; nay, I am convinced it is hard to avoid it, though one strove to separate the passion from its corresponding gestures' (James 1890: II, 464). Burke, in turn, claims to have learned this story from Jacob Spon's *Récherches d'antiquité* (Burke [1757] 1887: 213).

Experience

1 'the *coarser* emotions, grief, fear, rage, love, in which everyone recognizes a strong organic reverberation, . . . the *subtler* emotions, or of those whose organic reverberation is less obvious and strong' (James 1890: 449).

2 One year after the publication of 'What is an Emotion?', Danish physician Carl Georg Lange published *Om Sindsbevægelser*, which James presumably read in the German translation of 1887. Thus, despite working independently, these two scholars reached conclusions so similar to each other that they are often jointly referred to as the 'James-Lange theory'.

3 See, however, the criticism of Lange in James ([1894] 1994): 'Lange has laid far too great stress on the vaso-motor factor in his explanations' (205).

4 In this regard, Cannon (1927, 113–14) discusses Marañón's study which later inspired Schachter and Singer's experiment (see above, p. 50).

5 'The merely descriptive literature of the emotions is one of the most tedious parts of psychology. And not only is it tedious, but you feel that its subdivisions are to a great extent either fictitious or unimportant, and that its pretences to accuracy are a sham. . . . as far as "scientific psychology" of the emotions goes, I may have been surfeited by too much reading of classic works on the subject, but I should as lief read verbal descriptions of the shapes of the rocks on a New Hampshire farm as toil through them again' (James 1890: 448).

6 See also Lane et al. (1997), Mayberg et al. (1999), Critchley, Christopher and Dolan (2001); for more on this point see Damasio (2003: 96–105).

Alternatives and criticism

1 It is controversial whether there can be affective states without a particular object. Some argue that experiences such as depression, excitement or anxiety are not directed towards anything specific, while others believe that these too have a particular object, albeit of a very broad or general nature (e.g. existence, the world or the state of affairs). The distinction between emotions and moods is based precisely on whether or not it is possible to identify the particular object to which the affective state is directed. Of course, an 'object' should not be construed merely as a 'thing', but can encompass entities, persons, circumstances, and events (whether past, present or future, real or imaginary). In English, the 'object' of an emotion can be specified with a proposition ('I fear that p'), with an objective genitive

('I am proud of you'), with a direct object ('I love you'), with an instrument ('I am thrilled by your performance'), with specific circumstances ('I am moved at this thought') and so on.

2 This essay was presented at a conference in 2001 and appears in both Hatzimoysis (2003) and Solomon (2003), from which it is quoted here.

3 In fact, as we have seen, according to Lazarus appraisal processes are not necessarily deliberate and reflective, nor can be reduced to the formulation of a propositional judgement or assertion: Prinz's criticism that 'Lazarus's mistake is that he thinks core relational themes correspond to complex judgments in the head' (Prinz 2004a: 67) seems a little too harsh.

Debate II

1 Colombetti (2014) develops a critique of the dualism implicit in the distinction between emotion and cognition that the somatic marker hypothesis presupposes. Damasio's idea is that reasoning, as produced in the neocortical areas of the brain, is not sufficient to make good choices: it is also necessary that the different solutions contemplated theoretically be also accompanied by the relevant somatic states (i.e. by their corresponding emotions). Colombetti consequently points out that Damasio's model upholds a separation between emotion and cognition, identifying the former with bodily activity and the latter with the product of a more complex dimension of the mind, which as such would be limited to organisms endowed with a nervous system – and, more specifically, with a cerebral cortex.

2 For a comprehensive (though not very recent) survey of the experimental research that has been conducted to verify the somatic marker hypothesis, see Dunn, Dalgleish and Lawrence (2006). See Colombetti (2008) for a discussion of some of the theoretical problems connected with the somatic marker hypothesis.

3 Furthermore, as regards the negative correlation between the perception of risk and the perception of gains, see Fischoff et al. (1978); Slovic, Fischhoff and Lichtenstein (1980); Finucane et al. (2000).

Action

1 This is also the case with Dewey's interpreters, e.g. Garrison (2003: 412): 'Dewey *recognizes* Darwin makes a serious mistake; initially gestures,

tears, or laughter are simply acts, not expressions of significant meanings'
(Garrison 2003: 412; emphasis added).

2   See, however, the note added by Dewey: 'While Darwin's language is that of
the dependence of "expression" upon emotion, it is interesting to note that
so careful an observer has, in one place, anticipated and definitely stated
the discharge theory, *Expression of Emotions*, p. 239. (My references are
to the American edition.) "Most of our emotions are so closely connected
with their expression that they hardly exist if the body remains passive
– the nature of the expression depending in chief part on the nature of
the actions which have been habitually performed under this particular
state of mind." (Note in this latter phrase the assumption of the priority of
emotion; but the continuation is unambiguous in the other sense.) "A man,
for instance, may know that his life is in extremest peril, and may strongly
desire to save it; yet as Louis XVI said when surrounded by a fierce mob,
'Am I afraid? Feel my pulse.' So a man may intensely hate another, *but until
his bodily frame is affected* he cannot be said to be enraged"' (Dewey 1894:
554; Dewey's emphasis). In the end, it is not clear whether Dewey criticizes
Darwin outright or whether the charge of making too sharp a distinction
between emotion and expression is rather an argumentative strategy aimed
at emphasizing the 'agentive' nature of emotions.

Debate III

1   An earlier version of the argument presented in this section can be found in
Campeggiani (2020).

2   In fact, Walton does not deny that quasi-emotions involve physiological and
psychological states that cannot be phenomenologically distinguished from
real-life emotions; however, he does not believe that genuine emotions can
be identified on phenomenological grounds (Walton 1990: 195–6).

3   Matravers also compares emotions elicited by past historical events with
emotions towards fictional entities and argues that in both cases there is
a belief about the logical impossibility of interacting with the events in
question (though for different reasons: Matravers 1991: 34–5). On this basis,
Matravers has recently claimed that there is no 'paradox of fiction' in the first
place (Matravers 2014).

References

Armstrong, S. L., L. R. Gleitman and H. Gleitman (1983), 'What Some Concepts Might Not Be', *Cognition*, 13 (3): 263–308.

Arnold, M. B. (1960), *Emotion and Personality*, 2 vols, New York: Columbia University Press.

Avenanti, A., D. Bueti, G. Galati and S. M. Aglioti (2005), 'Transcranial Magnetic Stimulation Highlights the Sensorimotor Side of Empathy for Pain', *Nature Neuroscience*, 8: 955–60.

Bain, A. (1859), *Emotions and the Will*, London: John W. Parker and Son.

Baron-Cohen, S. (1995), *Mindblindness. An Essay on Autism and Theory of Mind*, Cambridge, MA: MIT Press.

Barrett, L. F. (2006), 'Are Emotions Natural Kinds?', *Perspectives on Psychological Science*, 1 (1): 28–58.

Barrett, L. F. (2017a), 'The Theory of Constructed Emotion: An Active Inference Account of Interoception and Categorization', *Social Cognitive and Affective Neuroscience*, 12 (1): 1–23.

Barrett, L. F. (2017b), *How Emotions are Made: The Secret Life of the Brain*, New York: Houghton Mifflin Harcourt.

Barrett, L. F. and M. Bar (2009), 'See It with Feeling: Affective Predictions During Object Perception', *Philosophical Transactions of the Royal Society of London (series B)*, 364: 1325–34.

Barrett, L. F. and J. A. Russell, eds (2015), *The Psychological Construction of Emotion*, New York: Guilford Press.

Barrett, L. F., R. Adolphs, S. Marsella, A. M. Martinez and S. D. Pollak (2019), 'Emotional Expressions Reconsidered: Challenges to Inferring Emotion from Human Facial Movements', *Psychological Science in the Public Interest*, 20 (1), 1–68.

Barrett, P., P. J. Gautrey, S. Herbert, D. Kohn and S. Smith, eds (2008), *Charles Darwin's Notebooks: 1836–1844*, Cambridge: Cambridge University Press.

Beach, K. (1988), 'The Role of External Mnemonic Symbols in Acquiring an Occupation', in M. M. Gruneberg, P. Morris and R. N. Sykes (eds), *Practical*

Aspects of Memory: Current Research and Issues, vol. 1: Memory of Everyday Life, 342–6, New York: Wiley.

Bechara, A. and A. R. Damasio (2005), 'The Somatic Marker Hypothesis: A Neural Theory of Economic Decision', *Games and Economic Behavior*, 52: 336–72.

Bechara, A., A. R. Damasio, H. Damasio and S. W. Anderson (1994), 'Insensitivity to Future Consequences Following Damage to Human Prefrontal Cortex', *Cognition*, 50: 7–15.

Bechara, A., D. Tranel, H. Damasio and A. R. Damasio (1996), 'Failure to Respond Autonomically to Anticipated Future Outcomes Following Damage to Prefrontal Cortex', *Cerebral Cortex*, 6 (2): 215–25.

Bell, C. (1802), *The Anatomy of the Brain, Explained in a Series of Engravings*, London: Longman and Rees.

Bell, C. (1806), *Essays on the Anatomy of Expression in Painting*, London: Longman, Hurst, Rees, and Orme.

Bell, C. (1811), 'Idea of a New Anatomy of the Brain', in N. Potter (ed.), *The Baltimore Medical and Philosophical Lycaeum I*, 303–18, Baltimore: George Hill.

Bell, C. (1824), *Essays on the Anatomy and Philosophy of Expression*, London: John Murray.

Benartzi, S. and R. Thaler (1995), 'Myopic Loss Aversion and the Equity Premium Puzzle', *The Quarterly Journal of Economics*, 110 (1): 73–92.

Berlin, B. and P. Kay (1969), *Basic Color Terms: Their Universality and Evolution*, Berkeley: University of California Press.

Bhalla, M. and D. R. Proffitt (1999), 'Visual-Motor Recalibration in Geographical Slant Perception', *Journal of Experimental Psychology: Human Perception and Performance*, 24 (4): 1076–96.

Boddice, R. (2016), *The Science of Sympathy. Morality, Evolution, and Victorian Civilization*, Urbana, Chicago, Springfield: University of Illinois Press.

Botvinick, M., A. P. Jha, L. M. Bylsma, S. A., P. E. Solomon and K. M. Prkachin (2005), 'Viewing Facial Expressions of Pain Engages Cortical Areas Involved in the Direct Experience of Pain', *NeuroImage*, 25 (1): 312–19.

Bourgeois, P. and U. Hess (2008), 'The Impact of Social Context on Mimicry', *Biological Psychology*, 77: 343–52.

Boyd, R. (1989), 'What Realism Implies and What It Does Not', *Dialectica*, 43: 5–29.

Browne, J. (1985), 'Darwin and the Expression of Emotions', in D. Kohn (ed.), *The Darwinian Heritage*, 307–26, Princeton: Princeton University Press.

Burke, E. ([1757] 1887), 'A Philosophical Enquiry into the Origin of our Ideas of the Sublime and Beautiful', in *The Works of the Right Honourable Edmund Burke in Twelve Volumes*, 67–262, London: John C. Nimmo.

Cairns, D. L. (2019), 'Introduction: Emotion History and the Classics', in Id. (ed.), *A Cultural History of Emotions in Antiquity*, London: Bloomsbury.

Campanella, T. (1637), *De Sensu Rerum et Magia*, Parisiis: Apud Ioannem du Bray.

Campeggiani, P. (2020), 'Nec Cogitare Sed Facere: The Paradox of Fiction at the Tribunal of Ancient Poetics', *Theoria*, 86 (6): 709–26.

Cannon, P. R., A. E. Hayes and S. P. Tipper (2009), 'An Electromyographic Investigation of the Impact of Task Relevance on Facial Mimicry', *Cognition and Emotion*, 23 (5): 918–29.

Cannon, W. B. (1927), 'The James-Lange Theory of Emotions: A Critical Examination and an Alternative Theory', *The American Journal of Psychology*, 39: 106–24.

Cannon, W. B., J. Lewis and S. Britton (1927), 'The Dispensability of the Sympathetic Division of the Autonomic Nervous System', *The Boston Medical and Surgical Journal*, 197 (13): 514–15.

Caracciolo, M. (2013), 'Narrative Space and Readers' Responses to Stories: A Phenomenological Account', *Style*, 47 (4): 425–44.

Caracciolo, M. (2014), 'Interpretation for the Bodies: Bridging the Gap', *Style*, 48 (3): 385–403.

Carroll, N. (1990), *The Philosophy of Horror or Paradoxes of the Heart*, London: Routledge.

Chartrand, T. L. and J. A. Bargh (1999), 'The Chameleon Effect: The Perception-Behavior Link and Social Interaction', *Journal of Personality and Social Psychology*, 76 (6): 893–910.

Clark, A. (2008), *Supersizing the Mind. Embodiment, Action, and Cognitive Extension*, New York: Oxford University Press.

Clark, A. and D. Chalmers (1998), 'The Extended Mind', *Analysis*, 58 (1): 7–19.

Clark, J. A. (2010), 'Relations of Homology between Higher Cognitive Emotions and Basic Emotions', *Biology & Philosophy*, 25 (1): 75–94.

Clore, G. L. and A. Ortony (2000), 'Cognition in Emotion: Always, Sometimes, or Never?', in R. D. Lane and L. Nadel (eds), *Cognitive Neuroscience of Emotion*, 24–61, New York: Oxford University Press.

Coleridge, S. T. ([1817] 2005), *Biographia Literaria. Or, Biographical Sketches of my Literary Life and Opinions, and Two Lay Sermons, I. The Statesman's Manual, II. Blessed Are Ye that Sow Beside All Waters*, Eugene: Wipf & Stock Publishers.

Colombetti, G. (2008), 'The Somatic Marker Hypotheses, and What the Iowa Gambling Task Does and Does Not Show', *The British Journal for the Philosophy of Science*, 59 (1): 51–71.

Colombetti, G. (2009), 'From Affect Programs to Dynamical Discrete Emotions', *Philosophical Psychology*, 22 (4); 407–25.

Colombetti, G. (2014), *The Feeling Body. Affective Science Meets the Enactive Mind*, Cambridge, MA: MIT Press.

Colombetti, G. (2016), 'Affective Incorporation', in J. Aaron Simmons and J. E. Hackett (eds), *Phenomenology for the Twenty-First Century*, 231–48, London: Palgrave Macmillan.

Colombetti, G. (2018), 'Enacting Affectivity', in A. Newen, L. De Bruin and S. Gallagher (eds), *The Oxford Handbook of 4E Cognition*, 571–88, Oxford: Oxford University Press.

Colombetti, G. and J. Krueger (2015), 'Scaffoldings of the Affective Mind', *Philosophical Psychology*, 28 (8): 1157–76.

Colombetti, G. and T. Roberts (2015), 'Extending the Extended Mind: The Case for Extended Affectivity', *Philosophical Studies*, 172: 1243–63.

Colombetti, G. and E. Thompson (2008), 'The Feeling Body: Towards an Enactive Approach to Emotion', in W. F. Overton, U. Müller and J. L. Newman (eds), *Developmental Perspectives on Embodiment and Consciousness*, 45–68, New York: Erlbaum.

Coplan, A. and P. Goldie (2011), *Empathy: Philosophical and Psychological Perspectives*, Oxford: Oxford University Press.

Costa A., A. Foucart, I. Arnon, M. Aparici and J. Apesteguia (2014), '"Piensa" Twice: On the Foreign Language Effect in Decision Making', *Cognition*, 130 (2): 236–54.

Cova, F. and F. Teroni (2016), 'Is the Paradox of Fiction Soluble in Psychology?', *Philosophical Psychology*, 29 (6): 930–42.

Crane, T. (2009), 'Intentionalism', in A. Beckerman and B. McLaughlin (eds), *The Oxford Handbook of Philosophy of Mind*, 474–93, New York: Clarendon Press.

Critchley, H. D., M. J. Christopher and R. J. Dolan (2001), 'Neuroanatomical Basis for First- and Second-Order Representations of Bodily States', *Nature Neuroscience*, 4: 207–12.

Crivelli, C. and A. J. Fridlund (2019), 'Inside-Out: From Basic Emotions Theory to the Behavioral Ecology View', *Journal of Nonverbal Behavior*, 43 (2): 161–94.

Cunningham, S. (1995), 'Dewey on Emotions: Recent Experimental Evidence', *Transactions of the Charles S. Peirce Society*, 31 (4): 865–74.

Currie, G. (1990), *The Nature of Fiction*, New York: Cambridge University Press.

Cyrano de Bergerac, H.-S. ([1657–1662] 1886), *Histoire comique des États et Empires de la Lune et du Soleil*, Paris: Ch. Delagrave; trans. by A. Lovell, *The Comical History of the States and Empires of the Worlds of the Moon and Sun written in French by Cyrano Bergerac*, London: Henry Rhodes.

Damasio, A. R. (1994), *Descartes' Error: Emotion, Reason, and the Human Brain*, New York: Putnam.

Damasio, A. R. (2003), *Looking for Spinoza. Joy, Sorrow, and the Feeling Brain*, London: William Heinemann.

Damasio, A. R., D. Tranel and H. Damasio (1991), 'Somatic Markers and the Guidance of Behavior: Theory and Preliminary Testing', in H. S. Levin, H. M. Eisenberg and A. L. Benton (eds), *Frontal Lobe Function and Dysfunction*, 217–29, New York: Oxford University Press.

Damasio, A. R., B. J. Everitt, D. Bishop, A. C. Roberts, T. W. Robbins and L. Weiskrantz (1996), 'The Somatic Marker Hypothesis and the Possible Functions of the Prefrontal Cortex', *Philosophical Transactions of the Royal Society of London (series B)*, 351 (1346): 1413–20.

Damasio, A. R., T. J. Grabowski, A. Bechara, H. Damasio, L. L. B. Ponto, J. Parvizi and R. D. Hichwa (2000), 'Subcortical and Cortical Brain Activity During the Feeling of Self-generated Emotion', *Nature Neuroscience*, 3 (10): 1049–56.

Dandoy, A. C. and A. G. Goldstein (1990), 'The Use of Cognitive Appraisal to Reduce Stress Reactions: A Replication', *Journal of Social Behavior and Personality*, 5 (4): 275–85.

Dardi, A. (1992), *Dalla Provincia all'Europa: L'influsso del Francese sull'Italiano tra il 1650 e il 1715*, Firenze: Le Lettere.

Darwin, C. (1859), *On the Origin of Species by Means of Natural Selection, or the Preservation of Favoured Races in the Struggle for Life*, London: Murray.

Darwin, C. (1871), *The Descent of Man, and Selection in Relation to Sex*, 2 vols, London: Murray.

Darwin, C. ([1872] 2009), *The Expression of the Emotions in Man and Animals*, Introduction, Afterword and Commentaries by Paul Ekman, New York: Oxford University Press.

Davis, J. I., A. Senghas, F. Brandt and K. N. Ochsner (2010), 'The Effects of BOTOX Injections on Emotional Experience', *Emotion*, 10 (3): 433–40.

De Sousa, R. (1987), *The Rationality of Emotion*, Cambridge, MA: MIT Press.

Decety, J., ed. (2011), *Empathy: From Bench to Bedside*, Cambridge, MA: MIT Press.

Decety, J. and W. Ickes (2009), *The Social Neuroscience of Empathy*, Cambridge, MA: MIT Press.

Deonna, J. A. (2006), 'Emotion, Perception and Perspective', *Dialectica*, 60 (1): 29–46.

Deonna, J. A. and F. Teroni (2012), *The Emotions. A Philosophical Introduction*, London, New York: Routledge.

Deonna, J. A. and F. Teroni (2014), 'In What Sense Are Emotions Evaluations?', in S. Roeser and C. Todd (eds), *Emotion and Value*, 15–31, Oxford: Oxford University Press.

Deonna, J. A. and F. Teroni (2015), 'Emotions as Attitudes', *Dialectica*, 69 (3): 293–311.

Dewey, J. (1894), 'The Theory of Emotion. (I) Emotional Attitudes', *The Psychological Review*, 1 (6): 553–69.

Dewey, J. (1895), 'The Theory of Emotion. (II) The Significance of Emotions', *The Psychological Review*, 2 (1): 13–32.

Dewey, J. (1896), 'The Reflex Arc Concept in Psychology', *The Psychological Review*, 3 (4): 357–70.

Di Gregorio, M. A., ed. (1990), *Charles Darwin's Marginalia I*, New York: Garland.

Di Paolo, E. (2005), 'Autopoiesis, Adaptivity, Teleology, Agency', *Phenomenology and the Cognitive Sciences*, 4 (4): 429–52.

Diels, H. and W. Kranz (1952), *Fragmente der Vorsokratiker*, Berlin: Weidmann.

Dimberg, U. (1982), 'Facial Reactions to Facial Expressions', *Psychophysiology*, 19: 643–7.

Dimberg, U. and M. Thunberg (1998), 'Rapid Facial Reactions to Emotional Facial Expressions', *Scandinavian Journal of Psychology*, 39 (1): 39–45.

Dimberg, U., M. Thunberg and K. Elmehed (2000), 'Unconscious Facial Reactions to Emotional Facial Expressions', *Psychological Science*, 11 (1): 86–9.

Dimberg, U., M. Thunberg and S. Grunedal (2002), 'Facial Reactions to Emotional Stimuli: Automatically Controlled Emotional Responses', *Cognition and Emotion*, 16 (4), 449–71.

Dixon, T. (2003), *From Passions to Emotions: The Creation of a Secular Psychological Category*, Cambridge: Cambridge University Press.

Donaldson, J. (2016), 'The Duck-Rabbit Ambiguous Figure', in F. Macpherson (ed.), *The Illusions Index*, https://www.illusionsindex.org/i/duck-rabbit (accessed 3 June 2022).

Donaldson, J. and F. Macpherson (2017), 'Müller-Lyer Illusion', in F. Macpherson (ed.), *The Illusions Index*, https://www.illusionsindex.org/ir/mueller-lyer (accessed 3 June 2022).

Dretske, F. (1981), *Knowledge and the Flow of Information*, Cambridge, MA: MIT Press.

Duclos, S. E. and J. D. Laird (2001), 'The Deliberate Control of Emotional Experience Through Control of Expressions', *Cognition and Emotion*, 15 (1): 27–56.

Duclos, S. E., J. D. Laird, E. Schneider, M. Sexter, L. Stern and O. van Lighten (1989), 'Emotion-Specific Effects of Facial Expressions and Postures on Emotional Experience', *Journal of Personality and Social Psychology*, 57 (1): 100–8.

Dunn, B. D., T. Dalgleish and A. D. Lawrence (2006), 'The Somatic Marker Hypothesis: A Critical Evaluation', *Neuroscience and Biobehavioral Reviews*, 30: 239–71.

Eibl-Eibesfeldt, I. (1973), 'The Expressive Behavior of the Deaf-And-Blind-Born', in M. Von Cranach and I. Vine (eds), *Social Communication and Movement*, 163–94, London: Academic.

Ekman, P. (1971), 'Universals and Cultural Differences in Facial Expressions of Emotion', in J. K. Cole (ed.), *Nebraska Symposium on Motivation*, 19: 207–83.

Ekman, P. (1980), 'Biological and Cultural Contributions to Body and Facial Movement in the Expression of Emotions', in A. Oksenberg Rorty (ed), *Explaining Emotions*, 73–102, Los Angeles: University of California Press.

Ekman, P. (1992), 'An Argument for Basic Emotions', *Cognition and Emotion*, 6 (3–4): 169–200.

Ekman, P. (1994), 'Strong Evidence for Universals in Facial Expressions: A Reply to Russell's Mistaken Critique', *Psychological Bulletin*, 115: 268–87.

Ekman, P. (1998), *Preface and Commentary, C. Darwin, The Expression of the Emotions in Man and Animals*, 3rd edn, London: Harper Collins.

Ekman, P. (1999), 'Basic Emotions', in T. Dalgleish and M. J. Power (eds), *Handbook of Cognition and Emotion*, 45–60, Chichester: Wiley.

Ekman, P. (2003), *Emotions Revealed*, New York: Times Books.

Ekman, P. and D. Cordaro (2011), 'What Is Meant by Calling Emotions Basic', *Emotion Review*, 3 (4): 364–70.

Ellsworth, P. C. (1994), 'William James and Emotion: Is a Century of Fame Worth a Century of Misunderstanding?', *Psychological Review*, 101 (2): 222–9.

Eslinger, P. J. and A. R. Damasio (1985), 'Severe Disturbance of Higher Cognition after Bilateral Frontal Lobe Ablation: Patient EVR', *Neurology*, 35 (12): 1731–41.

Fadiga, L., L. Fogassi, G. Pavesi and G. Rizzolatti (1995), 'Motor Facilitation During Action Observation: A Magnetic Stimulation Study', *Journal of Neurophysiology*, 73: 2608–11.

Fehr, B. and J. A. Russell (1984), 'Concept of Emotion Viewed From a Prototype Perspective', *Journal of Experimental Psychology*, 113 (3): 464–86.

Finucane, M. L., A. Alhakami, P. Slovic and S. M. Johnson (2000), 'The Affect Heuristic in Judgments of Risks and Benefits', *Journal of Behavioral Decision Making*, 13: 1–17.

Fischoff, B., P. Slovic, S. Lichtenstein, S. Read and B. Combs (1978), 'How Safe is Safe Enough? A Psychometric Study of Attitudes Towards Technological Risks and Benefits', *Policy Sciences*, 9: 127–52.

Flack, W. F. Jr., J. D. Lair and L. A. Cavallaro (1999), 'Separate and Combined Effects of Facial Expressions and Bodily Postures on Emotional Feelings', *European Journal of Social Psychology*, 29: 203–17.

Fodor, J. A. (1975), *The Language of Thought*, New York: Thomas Crowell.

Fodor, J. A. (1981), *Representations*, Cambridge, MA: MIT Press.

Fodor, J. A. (1983), *The Modularity of Mind*, Cambridge, MA: MIT Press.

Fodor, J. A. (2008), *LOT2: The Language of Thought Revisited*, Oxford: Clarendon Press.

Franks, D. D. (1991), 'Mead's and Dewey's Theory of Emotion and Contemporary Constructionism', *Journal of Mental Imagery*, 15 (1–2): 119–37.

Friend, S. (2016), 'Fiction and Emotion', in A. Kind (ed.), *The Routledge Handbook of Philosophy of Imagination*, 217–29, London, New York: Routledge.

Frijda, N. (1986), *The Emotions*, Cambridge: Cambridge University Press.

Frijda, N. (2007), *The Laws of Emotions*, Mahwah, NJ: Lawrence Erlbaum.

Frijda, N. (2010), 'Impulsive Action and Motivation', *Biological Psychology*, 84: 570–79.

Gallagher, S. (2005), *How The Body Shapes the Mind*, New York: Oxford University Press.

Gallagher, S. (2020), *Action and Interaction*, Oxford: Oxford University Press.

Gallagher, S. and D. D. Hutto (2007), 'Understanding Others Through Primary Interaction and Narrative Practice', in J. Zlatev, T. Racine, C. Sinha and E. Itkonen (eds), *The Shared Mind: Perspectives on Intersubjectivity*, 17–38, Amsterdam: John Benjamins.

Gallese, V. (2001), 'The 'Shared Manifold' Hypothesis: From Mirror Neurons to Empathy', *Journal of Consciousness Studies*, 8: 33–50.

Gallese, V. (2005), '"Being Like Me": Self-Other Identity, Mirror Neurons and Empathy', in S. Hurley and N. Chater (eds), *Perspectives on Imitation: From Neuroscience to Social Science, vol. 1: Mechanisms of Imitation and Imitation in Animals*, 101–18, Cambridge, MA: MIT Press.

Gallese, V. (2007), 'Before and Below 'Theory of Mind': Embodied Simulation and the Neural Correlates of Social Cognition', *Philosophical Transactions of the Royal Society of London (series B)*, 362 (1480): 659–69.

Gallese, V. and A. I. Goldman (1998), 'Mirror Neurons and the Simulation Theory of Mindreading', *Trends in Cognitive Sciences*, 2 (12): 493–501.

Gallese, V., L. Fadiga, L. Fogassi and G. Rizzolatti (1996), 'Action Recognition in the Premotor Cortex', *Brain*, 119: 593–609.

Garrison, J. (2003), 'Dewey's Theory of Emotions: The Unity of Thought and Emotion in Naturalistic Functional 'Co-ordination' of Behavior', *Transactions of the Charles S. Peirce Society*, 39 (3): 405–43.

Gerrig, R. J. (1993), *Experiencing Narrative Worlds: On the Psychological Activities of Reading*, New Haven: Yale University Press.

Gibson, J. J. (1979), *The Ecological Approach to Visual Perception*, Boston: Houghton Mifflin.

Goh, J. O. and D. C. Park (2009), 'Culture Sculpts the Perceptual Brain', *Progress in Brain Research*, (178): 95–111.

Goldie, P. (2000), *The Emotions: A Philosophical Introduction*, Oxford: Oxford University Press.

Goldie, P. (2004), 'Emotion, Feeling, and Knowledge of the World', in R. C. Solomon (ed.), *Thinking about Feeling: Contemporary Philosophers on Emotions*, 91–106, New York: Oxford University Press.

Goldman, A. I. (1989), 'Interpretation Psychologized', *Mind and Language*, 4: 161–85.

Goldman, A. I. (2006), *Simulating Minds: The Philosophy, Psychology, and Neuroscience of Mindreading*, New York: Oxford University Press.

Gopnik, A. and A. N. Meltzoff (1997), *Words, Thoughts and Theories*, Cambridge, MA: MIT Press.

Gopnik, A. and A. N. Meltzoff (2013), 'Learning about the Mind from Evidence: Children's Development of Intuitive Theories of Perception and Personality', in S. Baron-Cohen, H. Tager-Flusberg and M. V. Lombardo (eds), *Understanding Other Minds: Perspectives from Developmental Social Neuroscience*, 19–34, Oxford: Oxford University Press.

Gordon, R. M. (1986), 'Folk Psychology as Simulation', *Mind and Language*, 1: 158–71.

Green, M. C. and T. C. Brock (2002), 'In the Mind's Eye: Transportation-Imagery Model of Narrative Persuasion', in M. C. Green, J. J. Strange and T. C. Brock (eds), *Narrative Impact: Social and Cognitive Foundations*, 315–41, Mahwah, NJ: Lawrence Erlbaum Associates.

Griffiths, P. E. (1997), *What Emotions Really Are: The Problem of Psychological Categories*, Chicago: University of Chicago Press.

Griffiths, P. E. (2004), 'Is Emotion a Natural Kind?', in R. C. Solomon (ed.), *Thinking About Feeling: Contemporary Philosophers on Emotions*, 233–49, Oxford: Oxford University Press.

Griffiths, P. and A. Scarantino (2009), 'Emotions in the Wild: The Situated Perspective on Emotion', in P. Robbins and M. Aydede (eds), *The Cambridge Handbook of Situated Cognition*, 437–53, New York: Cambridge University Press.

Gross, D. M. (2010), 'Defending the Humanities with Charles Darwin's 'The Expression of the Emotions in Man and Animals' (1872)', *Critical Inquiry*, 37 (1): 34–59.

Gross, J. J. (1998), 'Antecedent- and Response-focused Emotion Regulation: Divergent Consequences for Experience, Expression, and Physiology', *Journal of Personality and Social Psychology*, 74 (1): 224–37.

Gross, J. J. and R. W. Levenson (1993), 'Emotional Suppression: Physiology, Self-Report, and Expressive Behavior', *Journal of Personality and Social Psychology*, 64 (6): 970–86.

Gross, J. J. and R. W. Levenson (1997), 'Hiding Feelings: The Acute Effects of Inhibiting Negative and Positive Emotion', *Journal of Abnormal Psychology*, 106 (1): 95–103.

Gutsell, J. N. and M. Inzlicht (2010), 'Empathy Constrained: Prejudice Predicts Reduced Mental Simulation of Actions During Observation of Out-Groups', *Journal of Experimental Social Psychology*, 46 (5): 841–5.

Hansen, T., M. Olkkonen, S. Walter and K. R. Gegenfurtner (2006), 'Memory Modulates Color Appearance', *Nature Neuroscience*, 9 (11): 1367–8.

Hatfield, E, J. T. Cacioppo and R. L. Rapson, eds (1994), *Emotional Contagion*, Cambridge: Cambridge University Press.

Hatfield, E., R. L. Rapson and L. Le Yen-Chi (2009), 'Emotional Contagion and Empathy', in J. Decety and W. Ickes (eds), *The Social Neuroscience of Empathy*, 9–30, Cambridge, MA: MIT Press.

Hatzimoysis, A., ed. (2003), *Philosophy and the Emotions*, Cambridge: Cambridge University Press.

Havas, D. A., A. M. Glenberg, K. A. Gutowski, M. J. Lucarelli, R. J. Davidson (2010), 'Cosmetic Use of Botulinum Toxin-A Affects Processing of Emotional Language', *Psychological Science*, 21 (7): 895–900.

Hayakawa, S., A. Costa, A. Foucart and B. Keysar (2016), 'Using a Foreign Language Changes Our Choices', *Trends in Cognitive Sciences*, 20 (11): 791–3.

Hess, U. and A. Fischer (2013), 'Emotional Mimicry as Social Regulation', *Personality and Social Psychology Review*, 17 (2): 142–57.

Hess, U. and A. Fischer (2014), 'Emotional Mimicry: Why and When We Mimic Emotions', *Social and Personality Psychology Compass*, 8 (2): 45–57.

Hickman, L. A., ed. (1996), *The Collected Works of John Dewey, 1882–1953: The Electronic Edition*, Charlottesville: InteLex Corporation, http://www.nlx.com /collections/133 (accessed 3 June 2022).

Hopkins, R. (2012), 'What Perky Did Not Show', *Analysis*, 72: 431–9.

Hufendiek, R. (2017), 'Affordances and The Normativity of Emotions', *Synthese*, 194: 4455–76.

Hurley, S. (1998), *Consciousness in Action*, Cambridge, MA: Harvard University Press.

Hurley, S. (2001), 'Perception and Action: Alternative Views', *Synthese*, 129 (1): 3–40.

Hutto, D. D. (2007), 'The Narrative Practice Hypothesis: Origins and Applications of Folk Psychology', *Royal Institute of Philosophy Supplement*, 60: 1–15.

Hutto, D. D. (2012), 'Truly Enactive Emotion', *Emotion Review*, 4 (2): 176–81.

Hutto, D. D. and E. Myin (2013), *Radicalizing Enactivism: Basic Minds Without Content*, Cambridge, MA: MIT Press.

Hutto, D. D. and E. Myin (2017), *Evolving Enactivism: Basic Minds Meet Content*, Cambridge, MA: MIT Press.

Irons, D. (1894), 'Professor James's Theory of Emotion', *Mind*, 3: 77–97.

Ivaz, L., A. Costa and J. A. Duñabeitia (2016), 'The Emotional Impact of Being Myself: Emotions and Foreign-Language Processing', *Journal of Experimental Psychology. Learning, Memory, and Cognition*, 42 (3): 489–96.

Izard, C. E. (1977), *Human Emotions*, Boston: Springer.

Izard, C. E. (1978), 'On the Ontogenesis of Emotions and Emotion-Cognition Relationships in Infancy', in M. Lewis and L. A. Rosenblum (eds), *The Development of Affect*, 389–413, New York: Plenum Press.

Izard, C. E. (2007), 'Basic Emotions, Natural Kinds, Emotion Schemas, and a New Paradigm', *Perspectives on Psychological Science*, 2 (3): 260–80.

Izard, C. E. (2011), 'Forms and Functions of Emotions: Matters of Emotion-Cognition Interactions', *Emotion Review*, 3 (4): 371–8.

Jackson, P. L., A. N. Meltzoff and J. Decety (2005), 'How Do We Perceive the Pain of Others? A Window into the Neural Processes Involved in Empathy', *NeuroImage*, 24 (3): 771–9.

Jajdelska, E., C. Butler, S. Kelly, A. McNeill and K. Overy (2010), 'Crying, Moving, and Keeping It Whole: What Makes Literary Description Vivid?', *Poetics Today*, 31 (3): 433–63.

James, W. (1884), 'What is an Emotion?', *Mind*, 9 (34): 188–205.

James, W. ([1890] 1981), *The Principles of Psychology: Volumes I and II*, Boston: Harvard University Press.

James, W. ([1894] 1994), 'The Physical Basis of Emotion', *Psychological Review*, 101 (2): 205–10.

Johnson, M. (1987), *The Body in the Mind: The Bodily Basis of Meaning, Imagination, and Reason*, Chicago: University of Chicago Press.

Kahneman, D. and A. Tversky (1979), 'Prospect Theory: An Analysis of Decision under Risk', *Econometrica*, 47 (2): 263–91.

Kahneman, D. and A. Tversky (1984), 'Choice, Values, and Frames', *American Psychologist*, 39: 341–50.

Kenny, A. (1963), *Action, Emotion, and Will*, London: Routledge.

Keysar, B., S. Hayakawa and A. Sun Gyu (2012), 'The Foreign-Language Effect: Thinking in a Foreign Tongue Reduces Decision Biases', *Psychological Science*, 23 (6): 661–8.

Konrad, E.-M., T. Petraschka and C. Werner (2018), 'The Paradox of Fiction: A Brief Introduction into Recent Developments, Open Questions, and Current Areas of Research, Including a Comprehensive Bibliography from 1975 to 2018', *Journal of Literary Theory*, 12 (2): 193–203.

Kosslyn, S. M. (1980), *Image and Mind*, Cambridge, MA: Harvard University Press.

Kosslyn, S. M. (1994), *Image and Brain: The Resolution of the Imagery Debate*, Cambridge, MA: MIT Press.

Kosslyn, S. M. (2005), 'Mental Images and the Brain', *Cognitive Neuropsychology*, 22: 333–47.

Kosslyn, S. M., G. Ganis and W. L. Thompson (2001), 'Neural Foundations of Imagery', *Nature Reviews Neuroscience*, 2: 635–42.

Kosslyn, S. M., W. L. Thompson, G. Ganis (2006), *The Case for Mental Imagery*, New York: Oxford University Press.

Kövecses, Z. (2000), *Metaphor and Emotion: Language, Culture, and Body in Human Feeling*, Cambridge: Cambridge University Press.

Kripke, S. A. (1980), *Naming and Necessity*, Cambridge, MA: Harvard University Press.

Krueger, J. (2014), 'Varieties of Extended Emotions', *Phenomenology and the Cognitive Sciences*, 13: 533–55.

Krueger, J. and S. Overgaard (2012), 'Seeing Subjectivity: Defending a Perceptual Account of Other Minds', *ProtoSociology: Consciousness and Subjectivity*, 47: 239–62.

Krueger, J. and T. Szanto (2016), 'Extended Emotions', *Philosophy Compass*, 11 (12): 863–78.

Kukkonen, K. (2014), 'Presence and Prediction: The Embodied Reader's Cascades of Cognition', *Style*, 48 (3): 367–84.

Kuzmičova, A. (2014), 'Literary Narrative and Mental Imagery: A View From Embodied Cognition', *Style*, 48 (3): 275–93.

Laird, J. D. (2007), *Feelings: The Perception of Self*, New York: Oxford University Press.

Lakoff, G. (1987), *Women, Fire, and Dangerous Things: What Categories Reveal About the Mind*, Chicago: University of Chicago Press.

Lakoff, G. (2016), 'Language and Emotion', *Emotion Review*, 8 (3): 269–73.

Lakoff, G. and M. Johnson (1980), *Metaphors We Live By*, Chicago: University of Chicago Press.

Lakoff, G. and M. Johnson (1999), *Philosophy in the Flesh: The Embodied Mind and Its Challenge to Western Thought*, New York: Basic Books.

Lakoff, G. and Z. Kövecses (1987), 'The Cognitive Model of Anger Inherent in American English', in Dorothy Holland and N. Quinn (eds), *Cultural Models in Language and Thought*, 195–221, Cambridge: Cambridge University Press.

Lane, R. D., E. M. Reiman, G. L. Ahern, G. E. Schwartz and R. J. Davidson (1997), 'Neuroanatomical Correlates of Happiness, Sadness, and Disgust', *The American Journal of Psychiatry*, 154 (7): 926–33.

Lange, C. G. (1885), *Om Sindsbevægelser. Et Psykofysiologisk Studie*, Copenhagen: Jacob Lunds.

Lanzetta, J. T., J. Cartwright-Smith and R. E. Eleck (1976), 'Effects of Nonverbal Dissimulation on Emotional Experience and Autonomic Arousal', *Journal of Personality and Social Psychology*, 33 (3): 354–70.

Larsen, J. T., G. G. Berntson, K. M. Poehlmann, T. A. Ito and J. T. Cacioppo (2008), 'The Psychophysiology of Emotion', in M. Lewis, J. Haviland-Jones and L. F. Barrett (eds), *Handbook of Emotions*, 3rd edn, 180–95, New York: Guilford Press.

Lazarus, R. S. (1966), *Psychological Stress and the Coping Process*, New York: McGraw-Hill.

Lazarus, R. S. (1982), 'Thoughts on the Relation Between Emotion and Cognition', *American Psychologist*, 37: 1019–24.

Lazarus, R. S. (1984), 'On the Primacy of Cognition', *American Psychologist*, 39: 124–9.

Lazarus, R. S. (1991), *Emotion and Adaptation*, New York: Oxford University Press.

Lazarus, R. S. (1999), 'The Cognition-Emotion Debate: A Bit of History', in T. Dalgleish and M. J. Power (eds), *Handbook of Cognition and Emotion*, 3–19, Chichester: Wiley.

Lazarus, R. S. (2001), 'Relational Meaning and Discrete Emotions', in K. R. Scherer, A. Schorr and T. Johnstone (eds), *Appraisal Processes in Emotion: Theory, Methods, Research*, 37–67, New York: Oxford University Press.

LeDoux, J. E. (1996), *The Emotional Brain*, New York: Simon & Schuster.

Leslie, A. M. (1987), 'Children's Understanding of the Mental World', in R. L. Gregory (ed.), *The Oxford Companion to the Mind*, 139–42, Oxford: Oxford University Press.

Leslie, A. M. (1994), 'Pretending and Believing: Issues in the Theory of ToMM', *Cognition*, 50: 211–38.

Leventhal, H. and K. R. Scherer (1987), 'The Relationship of Emotion to Cognition: A Functional Approach to a Semantic Controversy', *Cognition and Emotion*, 1 (1): 3–28.

Levinson, J. (1997), 'Emotion in Response to Art: A Survey of the Terrain', in M. Hjort and S. Laver (eds), *Emotion and the Arts*, 20–34, New York: Oxford University Press.

Lewis, M. D. (2005), 'Bridging Emotion Theory and Neurobiology Through Dynamical Systems Modeling', *Behavioral and Brain Sciences*, 28: 169–245.

Likowski, K. U., A. Mühlberger, B. Seibt, P. Pauli and P. Weyers (2008), 'Modulation of Facial Mimicry by Attitudes', *Journal of Experimental Social Psychology*, 44: 1065–72.

Lindquist, K. A. and L. F. Barrett (2008), 'Constructing Emotion: The Experience of Fear as a Conceptual Act', *Psychological Science*, 19 (9): 898–903.

Lindquist, K. A., M. Gendron, L. F. Barrett and B. C. Dickerson Bradford (2014), 'Emotion Perception, But Not Affect Perception, is Impaired with Semantic Memory Loss', *Emotion*, 14 (2): 375–87.

Liu, S., Q. Tan, S. Han, L. Wanyue, W. Xiujuan, G. Yetong, X. Qiang, Z. Xiaochu and Z. Lin (2019), 'The Language Context Effect in Facial

Expressions Processing and its Mandatory Characteristic', *Scientific Reports*, 9: 11045.

Livingston, P. (2019), 'Lange vs James on Emotion, Passion, and the Arts', *Royal Institute of Philosophy Supplement*, 85: 39–56.

Loewenstein, G. F., C. Hsee, E. U. Weber and N. Welch (2001), 'Risk as Feelings', *Psychological Bulletin*, 127 (2): 267–86.

Lyons, W. (1980), *Emotion*, Cambridge: Cambridge University Press.

MacCormack, J. K. and K. A. Lindquist (2017), 'Bodily Contributions to Emotion: Schachter's Legacy for a Psychological Constructionist View of Emotion', *Emotion Review*, 9 (1): 36–45.

MacLean, P. D. (1990), *The Triune Brain in Evolution: Role in Paleocerebral Functions*, New York: Plenum.

Macoir, J., C. Hudon, M.-P. Tremblay, R. Jr. Laforce and M. A. Wilson (2019), 'The Contribution of Semantic Memory to the Recognition of Basic Emotions and Emotional Valence: Evidence from the Semantic Variant of Primary Progressive Aphasia', *Social Neuroscience*, 14 (6): 705–16.

Marañon, G: (1924), 'Contribution à l'Étude de l'Action émotive de l'Adrénaline', *Revue Francaise d'Endocrinologie*, 2: 301–25.

Marchant, J., ed. (1916), *Alfred Russel Wallace: Letters and Reminiscences I*, London: Cassell.

Margolis, E. and S. Laurence, eds (1999), *Concepts: Core Readings*, Cambridge, MA: MIT Press.

Matravers, D. (1991), 'Who's Afraid of Virginia Woolf?', *Ratio*, 4: 25–37.

Matravers, D. (2014), *Fiction and Narrative*, New York: Oxford University Press.

Matsumoto, D. and B. Willingham (2009), 'Spontaneous Facial Expressions of Emotion of Congenitally and Noncongenitally Blind Individuals', *Journal of Personality and Social Psychology*, 96 (1): 1–10.

Mayberg, H. S., M. Liotti, S. K. Brannan, S. McGinnis, R. K. Mahurin, P. A. Jerabek, A. Silva, J. L. Tekell, C. C. Martin, J. L. Lancaster and P. T. Fox (1999), 'Reciprocal Limbic-Cortical Function and Negative Mood: Converging PET Findings in Depression and Normal Sadness', *The American Journal of Psychiatry*, 156 (5): 675–82.

Meltzoff A. N. (2007), '"Like Me": A Foundation for Social Cognition', *Developmental Science*, 10 (1): 126–34.

Moors, A. (2014), 'Flavors of Appraisal Theories of Emotion', *Emotion Review*, 6 (4): 303–7.

Morton, A. (1980), *Frames of Mind: Constraints on the Common-sense Conception of the Mental*, Oxford: Clarendon Press.

Murphy, F. C., I. Nimmo-Smith and A. D. Lawrence (2003), 'Functional Neuroanatomy of Emotions: A Meta-Analysis', *Cognitive, Affective, and Behavioral Neuroscience*, 3: 207–33.

Neal, D. T. and T. L. Chartrand (2011), 'Embodied Emotion Perception: Amplifying and Dampening Facial Feedback Modulates Emotion Perception Accuracy', *Social Psychology and Personality Science*, 2 (6): 673–8.

Neill, A. (1993), 'Fiction and the Emotions', *American Philosophical Quarterly*, 30 (1): 1–13.

Nell, V. (1988), *Lost in a Book: The Psychology of Reading for Pleasure*, New Haven: Yale University Press.

Newen, A., A. Welpinghus and G. Juckel (2015), 'Emotion Recognition as Pattern Recognition: The Relevance of Perception', *Mind and Language*, 30 (2): 187–208.

Niedenthal, P. M. (2007), 'Embodying Emotion', *Science*, 316: 1002–5.

Niedenthal, P. M., M. Brauer, J. B. Halberstadt and A. H. Inner-Ker (2001), 'When Did Her Smile Drop? Facial Mimicry and the Influences of Emotional State on the Detection of Change in Emotional Expression', *Cognition and Emotion*, 15: 853–64.

Noë, A. (2004), *Action in Perception*, Cambridge, MA: MIT Press.

Nussbaum, M. C. (2004), 'Emotions as Judgments of Value and Importance', in R. C. Solomon (ed.), *Thinking About Feeling: Contemporary Philosophers on Emotions*, 183–99, New York: Oxford University Press.

Page, J. W., P. Duhamel and M. A. Crognale (2011), 'ERP Evidence of Visualization at Early Stages of Visual Processing', *Brain and Cognition*, 75 (2): 141–6.

Panksepp, J. (1998), *Affective Neuroscience: The Foundations of Human and Animal Emotions*, New York: Oxford University Press.

Panksepp, J. (2007), 'Neurologizing the Psychology of Affects: How Appraisal-based Constructivism and Basic Emotion Theory can Coexist', *Perspectives on Psychological Science*, 2 (3): 281–96.

Panksepp, J. and D. Watt (2011), 'What is Basic about Basic Emotions? Lasting Lessons from Affective Neuroscience', *Emotion Review*, 3 (4): 387–96.

Pavlenko, A. (2012), 'Affective Processing in Bilingual Speakers: Disembodied Cognition?', *International Journal of Psychology*, 47 (6): 405–28.

Perky Cheves West, M. (1910), 'An Experimental Study of Imagination', *The American Journal of Psychology*, 21 (3): 422–52.

Pessoa, L. (2008), 'On the Relationship between Emotion and Cognition', in *Nature Reviews Neuroscience*, 9: 148–58.

Pessoa, L. (2010), 'Emotion and Cognition and the Amygdala: From "What Is It?" to "What's To Be Done?"', *Neuropsychologia*, 48: 3416–29.

Pessoa, L. (2013), *The Cognitive-Emotional Brain: From Interactions to Integration*, Cambridge, MA: MIT Press.

Peters, E. and P. Slovic (1996), 'The Role of Affect and Worldviews as Orienting Dispositions in the Perception and Acceptance of Nuclear Power', *Journal of Applied Social Psychology*, 26 (16): 1427–53.

Petrolini, V. and M. Viola (2020), 'Core Affect Dynamics: Arousal as a Modulator of Valence', *Review of Philosophy and Psychology*, 11: 783–801.

Plutchik, R. (2001), 'The Nature of Emotions', *American Scientist*, 89: 344–50.

Plutchik, R. and A. F. Ax (1967), 'A Critique of 'Determinants of Emotional State' by Schachter and Singer', *Psychophysiology*, 4: 79–82.

Prinz, J. J. (2004a), *Gut Reactions: A Perceptual Theory of Emotion*, New York: Oxford University Press.

Prinz, J. J. (2004b), 'Embodied Emotions', in R. C. Solomon (ed.), *Thinking About Feeling: Contemporary Philosophers on Emotions*, 44–60, New York: Oxford University Press.

Proffitt, D. R., M. Bhalla, R. Gossweiler and J. Midgett (1995), 'Perceiving Geographical Slant', *Psychonomic Bulletin & Review*, 2: 409–28.

Proffitt, D. R., S. H. Creem and W. D. Zosh (2001), 'Seeing Mountains in Mole Hills: Geographical-Slant Perception', *Psychological Science*, 12 (5): 418–23.

Radford, C. (1975), 'How Can We Be Moved by the Fate of Anna Karenina?', *Proceedings of the Aristotelian Society, Supplementary Volumes*, 49: 67–80.

Ratcliffe, M. (2005), 'William James on Emotion and Intentionality', *International Journal of Philosophical Studies*, 13 (2): 179–202.

Reisenzein, R., W.-U. Meyer and A. Schützwohl (1995), 'James and the Physical Basis of Emotion: A Comment on Ellsworth', *Psychological Review*, 102 (5): 757–61.

Richards, R. J. (2009), 'Darwin on Mind, Morals and Emotions', in J. Hodge and G. Radick (eds), *The Cambridge Companion to Darwin*, 96–119, Cambridge: Cambridge University Press.

Riskind, J. H. (1983), 'Nonverbal Expressions and the Accessibility of Life Experience Memories: A Congruence Hypothesis', *Social Cognition*, 2: 62–86.

Riskind, J. H. (1984), 'They Stoop to Conquer: Guiding and Self-Regulatory Functions of Physical Posture After Success and Failure', *Journal of Personality and Social Psychology*, 47: 479–93.

Rizzolatti, G. and M. Matelli (2003), 'Two Different Streams Form the Dorsal Visual System: Anatomy and Functions', *Experimental Brain Research*, 153 (2): 146–57.

Rizzolatti, G., L. Fadiga, V. Gallese and L. Fogassi (1996), 'Premotor Cortex and the Recognition of Motor Actions', *Cognitive Brain Research*, 3, 131–41.

Roberts, R. C. (2003), *Emotions: An Essay in Aid of Moral Psychology*, Cambridge: Cambridge University Press.

Rosch, E. (1978), 'Principles of Categorization', in E. Rosch and B. Lloyd (eds), *Cognition and Categorization*, 27–48, Hillsdale, NJ: Lawrence Erlbaum Associates.

Rosch, E. and C. B. Mervis (1975), 'Family Resemblances: Studies in the Internal Structure of Categories', *Cognitive Psychology*, 7 (4): 573–605.

Rosenzweig, M, M. S. Breedlove and N. V. Watson (2005), *Biological Psychology: An Introduction to Behavioral and Cognitive Neuroscience*, Sunderland, MA: Sinauer Associates.

Rossi, M. and C. Tappolet (2018), 'What Kind of Evaluative States Are Emotions? The Attitudinal Theory vs. the Perceptual Theory of Emotions', *Canadian Journal of Philosophy*, 49 (4): 544–63.

Russell, J. A. (1991), 'The Contempt Expression and the Relativity Thesis', *Motivation and Emotion*, 15: 149–68.

Russell, J. A. (1994), 'Is There Universal Recognition of Emotion from Facial Expression? A Review of the Cross-Cultural Studies', *Psychological Bulletin*, 115 (1): 102–41.

Russell, J. A. (1995), 'Facial Expressions of Emotion: What Lies Beyond Minimal Universality?', *Psychological Bulletin*, 118 (3): 379–91.

Russell, J. A. (2003), 'Core Affect and the Psychological Construction of Emotion', *Psychological Review*, 110 (1): 145–72.

Russell, J. A. (2012), 'Introduction to Special Section: On Defining Emotion', *Emotion Review*, 4 (4): 337.

Ryan, M.-L. (1991), *Possible Worlds, Artificial Intelligence, and Narrative Theory*, Bloomington: Indiana University Press.

Salmela, M. (2011), 'Can Emotion Be Modelled on Perception?', *Dialectica*, 65 (1): 1–29.

Scarantino, A. (2012), 'How to Define Emotions Scientifically', *Emotion Review*, 4 (4): 358–68.

Scarantino, A. (2014), 'The Motivational Theory of Emotions', in J. D'Arms and D. Jacobson (eds), *Moral Psychology and Human Agency*, 156–85, Oxford: Oxford University Press.

Scarantino, A. (2015), 'Basic Emotions, Psychological Construction and the Problem of Variability', in L. F. Barrett and J. A. Russell (eds), *The Psychological Construction of Emotion*, 334–76, New York: Guilford Press.

Scarantino, A (2016), 'The Philosophy of Emotions and Its Impact on Affective Science', in L. F. Barrett, M. Lewis and J. Haviland-Jones (eds), *Handbook of Emotions*, 4th edn, 3–48, New York: Guilford Press.

Scarantino, A. (2017), 'Do Emotions Cause Actions, And If So How?', *Emotion Review*, 9 (4): 326–34.

Schachter, S. and J. Singer (1962), 'Cognitive, Social, and Physiological Determinants of Emotional State', *Psychological Review*, 69: 379–99.

Schargel, D. and J. J. Prinz (2017), 'An Enactivist Theory of Emotional Content', in H. Naar and F. Teroni (eds), *The Ontology of Emotions*, 110–29, Cambridge: Cambridge University Press.

Scheler, M. ([1923] 1973), *Wesen und Formen der Sympathie*, Bern, München: Francke Verlag.

Scherer, K. R. (1984), 'On the Nature and Function of Emotion: A Component Process Approach', in K. R. Scherer and P. Ekman (eds), *Approaches to Emotion*, 293–317, Hillsdale: Lawrence Erlbaum Associates.

Scherer, K. R. (2001), 'Appraisal Considered as a Process of Multilevel Sequential Checking', in K. R. Scherer, A. Schorr and T. Johnstone (eds.), *Appraisal Processes in Emotion: Theory, Methods, Research*, 92–120, New York: Oxford University Press.

Scherer, K. R. (2009), 'The Dynamic Architecture of Emotion: Evidence for the Component Process Model', *Cognition and Emotion*, 23 (7): 1307–51.

Scherer, K. R., A. Schorr and T. Johnstone, eds (2001), *Appraisal Processes in Emotion: Theory, Methods, Research*, New York: Oxford University Press.

Searle, J. (1983), *Intentionality: An Essay in the Philosophy of Mind*, New York: Cambridge University Press.

Segal, S. J. (1971), 'Processing of the Stimulus in Imagery and Perception', in Id. (ed.), *Imagery: Current Cognitive Approaches*, 73–100, New York: Academic Press.

Segal, S. J. (1972), 'Assimilation of a Stimulus in the Construction of an Image: The Perky Effect Revisited', in P. W. Sheenan (ed.), *The Function and Nature of Imagery*, 203–30, New York, London: Academic Press.

Sell, A., L. Cosmides and J. Tooby (2014), 'The Human Anger Face Evolved to Enhance Cues of Strength', *Evolution and Human Behavior*, 35 (5): 425–9.

Im Shin, H. and J. Kim (2017), 'Foreign Language Effect and Psychological Distance', *Journal of Psycholinguistic Research*, 46 (6): 1339–52.

Shiv, B., G. Loewenstein and A. Bechara (2005a), 'The Dark Side of Emotion in Decision-Making: When Individuals With Decreased Emotional Reactions Make More Advantageous Decisions', *Cognitive Brain Research*, 23: 85–92.

Shiv, B., G. Loewenstein, A. Bechara, H. Damasio and A. R. Damasio (2005b), 'Investment Behavior and the Negative Side of Emotion', *Psychological Science*, 15 (6): 435–9.

Simons, D. J. and C. F. Chabris (1999), 'Gorillas in Our Midst: Sustained Inattentional Blindness for Dynamic Events', *Perception*, 28 (9): 1059–74.

Slovic, P., B. Fischhoff and S. Lichtenstein (1980), 'Facts and Fears: Understanding Perceived Risk', in R. C. Schwing and W. A. Albers (eds), *Societal Risk Assessment*, 181–216, *General Motors Research Laboratories*, Boston: Springer.

Slovic, P., M. L. Finucane, E. Peters and D. G. MacGregor (2007), 'The Affect Heuristic', *European Journal of Operational Research*, 177: 1333–52.

Solomon, R. C. ([1976] 1993), *The Passions: Emotions and the Meaning of Life*, Indianapolis: Hackett.

Solomon, R. C. (2003), *Not Passion's Slave: Emotion and Choice*, New York: Oxford University Press.

Sonnby-Borgström, M. (2002), 'Automatic Mimicry Reactions as Related to Differences in Emotional Empathy', *Scandinavian Journal of Psychology*, 43: 433–43.

Stecker, R. (2011), 'Should We Still Care About the Paradox of Fiction?', *British Journal of Aesthetics*, 51 (3): 295–308.

Stepper, S. and F. Strack (1993), 'Proprioceptive Determinants of Emotional and Nonemotional Feelings', *Journal of Personality and Social Psychology*, 64: 211–20.

Strack, F., L. L. Martin and S. Stepper (1988), 'Inhibiting and Facilitating Conditions of the Human Smile: A Nonobtrusive Test of the Facial Feedback Hypothesis', *Journal of Personality and Social Psychology*, 54 (5): 768–77.

Sznycer, D., L. Al-Shawaf, Y. Bereby-Meyer, O. S. Curry, D. De Smet, E. Ermer, S. Kim, S. Kim, N. P. Li, M. F. Lopez Seal, J. McClung, J. O, Y. Ohtsubo, T. Quillien, M. Schaub, A. Sell, F. van Leeuwen, L. Cosmides and J. Tooby (2017a), 'Cross-Cultural Regularities in the Cognitive Architecture of Pride', *Proceedings of the National Academy of Sciences*, 114 (8): 1874–9.

Sznycer, D., L. Cosmides and J. Tooby (2017b), 'Adaptationism Carves Emotions At Their Functional Joints', *Psychological Inquiry*, 28 (1): 56–62.

Sznycer, D., M. F. Lopez Seal, A. Sell, J. Lim, R. Porat, S. Shalvi, E. Halperin, L. Cosmides and J. Tooby (2017c), 'Support for Redistribution is Shaped by Compassion, Envy, and Self-interest, But Not a Taste for Fairness', *Proceedings of the National Academy of Sciences*, 114 (31): 8420–5.

Tappolet, C. (2016); *Emotions, Values, and Agency*, Oxford: Oxford University Press.

Teroni, F. (2007), 'Emotions and Formal Objects', *Dialectica*, 61 (3): 395–415.

Teroni, F. (2019), 'Emotion, Fiction and Rationality', *British Journal of Aesthetics*, 59 (2): 113–28.

Thayer, S. (1980), 'The Effect of Facial Expression Sequence Upon Judgments of Emotion', *The Journal of Social Psychology*, 111 (2): 305–6.

Thompson, E. (2007), *Mind in Life: Biology, Phenomenology, and the Sciences of Mind*, Cambridge, MA: Harvard University Press.

Tomkins, S. ([1961-1991] 2008), *Affect Imagery Consciousness. The Complete Edition: Two Volumes*, New York: Springer.

Tooby, J. and L. Cosmides (2008), 'The Evolutionary Psychology of the Emotions and their Relationship to Internal Regulatory Variables', in M. Lewis, J. Haviland-Jones and L. F. Barrett (eds), *Handbook of Emotions*, 3rd edn, 114–37, New York: Guilford Press.

Troscianko, E. T. (2014a), 'Reading Kafka Enactively', *Paragraph*, 37: 15–31.

Troscianko, E. T. (2014b), *Kafka's Cognitive Realism*, New York, London: Routledge.

Tullman, K. and W. Buckwalter (2014), 'Does the Paradox of Fiction Exist?', *Erkenn*, 79: 779–96.

Tversky, A. and D. Kahneman (1974), 'Biases in Judgments Reveal Some Heuristics of Thinking Under Uncertainty', *Science*, 185 (4157): 1124–31.

Tversky, A. and D. Kahneman (1981), 'The Framing of Decisions and the Psychology of Choice', *Science*, 211 (4481): 453–8.

Van der Gaag, C., R. B. Minderaa and C. Keysers (2007), 'Facial Expressions: What the Mirror Neuron System Can and Cannot Tell Us', *Social Neuroscience*, 2 (3–4): 179–222.

Van der Schalk, J., A. Fischer, B. Doosje, D. Wigboldus, S. Hawk, M. Rotteveel and U. Hess (2011), 'Congruent and Incongruent Responses to Emotional Displays of Ingroup and Outgroup', *Emotion*, 11: 286–98.

Van Wyhe, J., ed. (2002), *The Complete Work of Charles Darwin*, http://darwin-online.org.uk (accessed 3 June 2022).

Varela, F. J., E. Thompson and E. Rosch (1991), *The Embodied Mind: Cognitive Science and Human Experience*, Cambridge, MA: MIT Press.

Vritčka, P., D. Sander and P. Vuilleumier (2011), 'Effects of Emotion Regulation Strategy on Brain Responses to the Valence and Social Content of Visual Scenes', *Neuropsychologia*, 49 (5): 1067–82.

Walton, K. L. (1978), 'Fearing Fictions', *Journal of Philosophy*, 75 (1): 5–27.

Walton, K. L. (1990), *Mimesis as Make-Believe: On the Foundations of the Representational Arts*, Cambridge, MA: Harvard University Press.

Watson, J. B. (1919), *Psychology From the Standpoint of a Behaviorist*, Philadelphia: Lippincott.

Weyers, P., A. Mkühlberger, A. Kund, U. Hess and P. Pauli (2009), 'Modulation of Facial Reactions to Avatar Emotional Faces by Non-Conscious Competition Priming', *Psychophysiology*, 46: 328–35.

Wicker, B., C. Keysers, J. Plailly, J.-P. Royet, V. Gallese and G. Rizzolatti (2003), 'Both of Us Disgusted in My Insula: The Common Neural Basis of Seeing and Feeling Disgust', *Neuron*, 40 (3): 655–64.

Widen, S. C. (2016), 'The Development of Children's Concepts of Emotion', in L. F. Barrett, M. Lewis and J. Haviland-Jones (eds), *Handbook of Emotions*, 4th edn, 307–18, New York: Guilford Press.

Widen, S. C. and J. A. Russell (2008), 'Children Acquire Emotion Categories Gradually', *Cognitive Development*, 23: 291–312.

Widen, S. C. and J. A. Russell (2010), 'Descriptive and Prescriptive Definitions of Emotion', *Emotion Review*, 2 (4): 377–8.

Wilcox, K. and J. D. Laird (2000), 'The Impact of Media Images of Super-slender Women on Women's Self-Esteem: Identification, Social Comparison, and Self-Perception', *Journal of Research in Personality*, 32 (2): 278–86.

Winawer, J., N. Witthoft, M. C. Frank, L. Wu, A. R. Wade, L. Boroditsky (2007), 'Russian Blues Reveal Effects of Language on Color Discrimination', *Proceedings of the National Academy of Sciences*, 104 (19): 7780–5.

Wittgenstein, L. (1953), *Philosophical Investigations*, ed. G. E. M. Anscombe, New York: The MacMillan Company.

Wittgenstein, L. ([1967] 2007), *Zettel*, ed. G. E. M. Anscombe and G. H. von Wright, Berkeley, Los Angeles: University of California Press.

Worcester, W. J. (1893), 'Observations on Some Points in James's Psychology. II: Emotion', *The Monist*, 3 (2): 285–98.

Wundt, W. (1891), 'Zum Lehre von den Gemüthsbewegungen', *Philosophische Studien*, 6: 335–93.

Xu, X., X. Zuo, X. Wang and S. Han (2009), 'Do You Feel My Pain? Racial Group Membership Modulates Empathic Neural Responses', *Journal of Neuroscience*, 29 (26): 8525–9.

Zahavi, D. (2011), 'Empathy and Direct Social Perception: A Phenomenological Proposal', *Review of Philosophy and Psychology*, 2: 541–58.

Zajonc, R. (1980), 'Feeling and Thinking: Preferences Need No Inferences', *American Psychologist*, 35: 151–75.

Zajonc, R. (1984), 'On the Primacy of Affect', *American Psychologist*, 39: 117–23.

Index

200

Index